Basic Skills for the

TOEFL® iBT

Iain Donald Binns
Micah Sedillos

Compass Publishing

Listening

1

Basic Skills for the TOEFL® iBT 1
Listening

Iain Donald Binns | Micah Sedillos

© 2008 Compass Publishing

Project Editor: Liana Robinson
Acquisitions Editor: Emily Page
Content Editor: Erik Custer
Copy Editor: Michael Jones
Contributing Writers: Moraig Macgillivray, Jeff Zeter
Consultants: Lucy Han, Chanhee Park
Cover/Interior Design: Dammora Inc

email: info@compasspub.com
http://www.compasspub.com

ISBN: 978-1-59966-151-3

10 9 8 7 6 5 4 3
10 09 08

Photo Credits
pp. 40, 44, 50, 54, 64, 74, 77, 78, 88, 98, 122, 148 © iStock International Inc.
pp. 24, 34, 80, 82, 92, 102, 112, 118, 128, 142, 145, 152 © Shutterstock, Inc.
pp. 20, 30, 60, 70, 84, 108, 132, 138,140, 150 © Jupiterimages Corporation

Contents

Introduction to the TOEFL® iBT

What is the TOEFL® test?

The TOEFL® iBT test (Test of English as a Foreign Language Internet-based test) is designed to assess English proficiency in non-native speakers who want to achieve academic success as well as effective communication. It is not meant to test academic knowledge or computer ability; therefore, questions are always based on material found in the test.

The TOEFL® iBT test is divided into four sections:
- Reading
- Speaking
- Listening
- Writing

TOEFL® Scores

TOEFL® scores can be used for:
- Admission into university or college where instruction is in English
- Employers or government agencies who need to determine a person's English ability
- English-learning institutes who need to place students in the appropriate level of English instruction

It is estimated that about 4,400 universities and other institutions require a certain TOEFL® test score for admission.

The exact calculation of a TOEFL® test score is complicated and not necessary for the student to understand. However, it is helpful to know that:
- Each section in the Internet-based test is worth 30 points
- The highest possible score on the iBT is 120 points
- Each institution will have its own specific score requirements

✲ It is very important to check with each institution individually to find out what its admission requirements are.

Registering for the TOEFL® iBT

Students who wish to take the TOEFL® test must get registration information. Registration information can be obtained online at the ETS website. The Internet address is www.ets.org/toefl.

The website provides information such as:
- testing locations
- identification requirements
- registration information
- costs
- other test preparation material
- test center locations

This information will vary depending on the country in which you take the test. Be sure to follow the requirements carefully. If you do not have the proper requirements in order, you may not be able to take the test. Remember that if you register online, you will need to have your credit card information ready.

Introduction to the Listening Section of the TOEFL® iBT

In the listening section of the TOEFL® test, you will hear a variety of conversations and lectures, each of which lasts from 3–6 minutes. A total of six listening passages will be presented. After each passage, you will then be asked to answer 5–6 questions about what you heard. These questions are designed to test your ability to
- recognize and understand the main idea
- determine factual information
- determine inference

You will not be asked questions regarding vocabulary or sentence structure. You will not be permitted to see the questions until after you have listened to the conversation or lecture. Although some questions will replay part of the conversation or lecture, you cannot choose to listen to it again while answering the questions. You do not need any previous knowledge on the topic in order to answer the questions correctly.

Passage Types

1. Conversations—two people discussing a campus-related problem, issue, or process
2. Lectures—a professor speaking a monologue, presenting information related to an academic topic
3. Classroom interaction—similar to the lecture passage type, but with some interaction between the professor and one or more students

Listening Question Types

Most questions will be normal multiple-choice. However, the other types are
- multiple-choice questions with more than one answer
- replay questions where the test taker will listen to part of the conversation again before choosing the correct answer
- questions that asks the test taker to put events or steps of a process in order
- questions that require the test taker to match text or objects to a category

The following list explains the types and number of each question per listening passage on the TOEFL® iBT test. Questions may not appear in this order.

Question Type	Number	Description
Main Idea	1	Choose the best phrase or sentence
Detail	1-2	Choose the statement that is true according to the listening passage
Function	1-2	Choose the answer that explains why the speaker has said something
Attitude	1-2	Choose the answer that describes the speakers emotion, attitude, or opinion
Organization	0-1	Explain how or why the speaker communicated certain information
Content	0-1	Select the answers that feature points from the listening passage

Most questions are worth 1 point each; however, some may be worth more.

Test management:

- A visual image will be given on the screen to allow test takers to recognize each speaker's role and the context of the conversation.
- Before you begin the listening section, listen to the headset directions. Pay particular attention to how you change the volume. It is very important that you be able to hear clearly during the listening section of the test.
- If you miss something that is said in a conversation or lecture, do not panic. Forget about it, and simply keep listening. Even native speakers do not hear everything that is said.
- Note-taking during the lecture is permitted. Paper will be provided by the test supervisor. These notes can be studied while answering the questions.
- Like the reading section, questions cannot be viewed until after the lecture/conversation has been completed.
- You must answer each question as it appears. You can NOT return to any questions later.
- Do not leave any question unanswered. You are NOT penalized for guessing an answer.

Introduction to the *Basic Skills for the TOEFL® iBT* series

Basic Skills for the TOEFL® iBT is a 3-level, 12-book test preparation series designed for beginning-level students of the TOEFL® iBT. Over the course of the series, students build on their current vocabulary to include common TOEFL® and academic vocabulary. They are also introduced to the innovative questions types found on the TOEFL® iBT, and are provided with practice of TOEFL® iBT reading, listening, speaking, and writing passages, conversations, lectures, and questions accessible to students of their level.

Basic Skills for the TOEFL® iBT enables students to build on both their language skills and their knowledge. The themes of the passages, lectures, and questions cover the topics often seen on the TOEFL® iBT. In addition, the independent topics, while taking place in a university setting, are also accessible to and understood by students preparing to enter university. The academic topics are also ones that native speakers study.

Students accumulate vocabulary over the series. Vocabulary learned at the beginning of the series will appear in passages and lectures later in the book, level, and series. Each level gets progressively harder. The vocabulary becomes more difficult, the number of vocabulary words to be learned increases, and the passages, conversations, and lectures get longer and increase in level. By the end of the series, students will know all 570 words on the standard Academic Word List (AWL) used by TESOL and have a solid foundation in and understanding of the TOEFL® iBT.

Not only will *Basic Skills for the TOEFL® iBT* start preparing students for the TOEFL® iBT, but it will also give students a well-rounded basis for either further academic study in English or further TOEFL® iBT study.

Introduction to the *Basic Skills for the TOEFL® iBT* Listening Book
This is the first listening book in the *Basic Skills for the TOEFL® iBT* series. The student will listen to two conversations and two lectures in each unit. The conversations will be between either a student and a university employee or a student and a professor. The lectures will be on the topics that the student was introduced to in the first reading book.

Each unit is separated into seven sections:

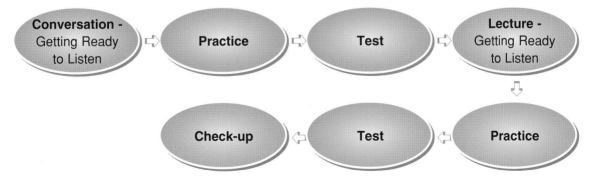

The following will outline the activities and aims of each section.

Conversation - Getting Ready to Listen

Key Vocabulary and TOEFL® Vocabulary

Students begin by studying the vocabulary they will encounter in the following passage. **TOEFL® Vocabulary** is the words that have been found to appear most often in TOEFL® preparation materials or are Academic Word List (AWL) words. TOEFL® Vocabulary is the most important words for the student to learn in order to build their vocabulary before further TOEFL® study. **Key Vocabulary** is the other words that are important for the student to know in order to understand the conversation that will follow.

TOEFL® Question Types

In this part, students will become familiar with
- one of the question types that appear in the TOEFL® iBT listening section
- the common wording of this question type in the conversation section
- the aims of the question type
- the strategy for identifying the question type

Becoming familiar with the question types is important for the student, as it will help them answer the questions appropriately. Therefore, the student will be less likely to get confused or distracted by the wording of TOEFL® questions.

Over the course of the book, all the listening question types will be covered.

Practice

Conversation

Students listen to the first part of the first conversation. They then answer two multiple-choice questions, which help the student to identify the main idea and purpose of the conversation. Listening to only the first part of the conversation enables the students to practice listening for main ideas without having to focus on the details.

Note-taking

Students now listen to the full conversation. It contains the vocabulary words learned on the previous page, so there should be very few words that student is unfamiliar with. Although the conversation is based in a university, it is accessible to and understood by students preparing to enter university. This helps students become used to listening to university-situated conversations but at a level they can understand.

Students take notes as they listen to the conversation. The notes are guided so that the student only has to fill in the parts that are missing. This introduces the students to a common way of conversation note-taking. This enables them to become used to thinking about not only the passage in general but also specific details and how the main idea is developed throughout the conversation.

TOEFL® Questions

The next page gives students the opportunity to practice the question types they were introduced to in this unit and the previous unit. There will be two of the question type learned in this unit and one from the previous unit. They will be worded in the same way as they are in the real TOEFL® test.

TOEFL® Vocabulary Practice

The next part is sentences using the TOEFL® vocabulary the student learned at the beginning of the section. This helps students practice the words in context.

Test

The test contains the second conversation of the unit. It is similar to the real TOEFL® test, but at an appropriate level for the student. It gives the student the opportunity to practice many question types at the same time. The test passage also uses many of the vocabulary words learned at the beginning of the section.

Lecture - Getting Ready to Listen

Key Vocabulary and TOEFL® Vocabulary

This is the Key Vocabulary and TOEFL® Vocabulary they will encounter in following lecture. See the conversation description for further details.

TOEFL® Question Type

In this part, students will become familiar with
- one of the question types that appear in the TOEFL® iBT Listening section
- the common wording of this question type in the lecture section
- the aims of the question type
- the strategy for identifying the question type

See the conversation description for further details.

Practice

Lecture

Students listen to the first part of the first lecture. They then answer three multiple-choice questions, which help the student to identify the main idea, purpose, and organization of the lecture. The fourth multiple-choice question asks the student to identify the best note-taking diagram to use for the lecture. Students can look at the answers to the previous three multiple-choice questions to help them decide. Listening to only the first part of the lecture enables the students to practice listening for main ideas and structure without having to focus on the details.

Note-taking

Students now draw the note-taking diagram they chose in the previous question. They can then insert the information from questions 1 and 2. They will then listen to the full lecture and fill in the rest of the notes. The lecture contains the vocabulary words learned on the previous page, so there should be very few words that student is unfamiliar with.

Using the designated note-taking diagram introduces the students to a common way of note-taking for the type of lecture. This enables them to become used to different ways to take notes and how to identify the lecture's specific details and how its main idea is developed and organized.

TOEFL® Questions

The next page gives students the opportunity to practice the question types they were introduced to in this unit and the previous unit. There will be two of the question type learned in this unit and one from the previous unit. They will be worded in the same way as they are in the real TOEFL® test.

TOEFL® Vocabulary Practice

The next part is sentences using the TOEFL® vocabulary learned at the beginning of the lecture section. This helps students practice the words in context.

Test

The test contains the second lecture of the unit. It is longer than the first lecture, but it will build on its content. This test is similar to the real TOEFL® test, but at an appropriate level for the student. It gives the student the opportunity to practice many question types at the same time. The test passage also uses many of the vocabulary words learned at the beginning of the lecture section.

Check-up

Question Type Review

These questions check the student understands the aim of question type that was focused on throughout the unit.

Key Vocabulary Practice

This part is sentences using the Key vocabulary the student learned over the course of the unit. This helps students practice the words in context.

Introduction to Note-taking Diagrams for Listening Lectures

The note-taking diagrams shown below are used throughout the book. This explains the diagrams a little further.

Units 1 and 7
Concept Defining Diagram

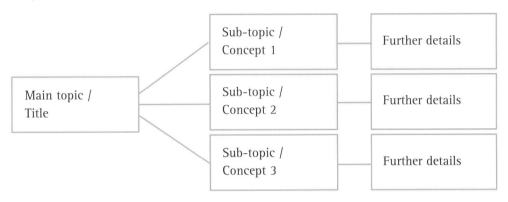

This note-taking diagram is used to define the concepts of an overall topic. There can be many or only a few boxes coming off the main topic. There may also be another level that contains further details. In this book, there will only be a few subtopics / concepts and a few further details.

Units 2 and 8
Venn Diagram

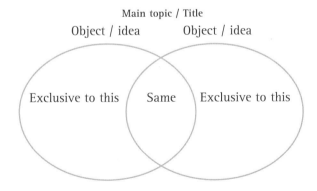

This note-taking diagram is used to compare and contrast objects and ideas. They are usually related under a common heading. There can be two or three circles. In this book, there will only be two things compared, thus only two circles will be needed.

Units 3 and 9
Problem and Solution Diagram

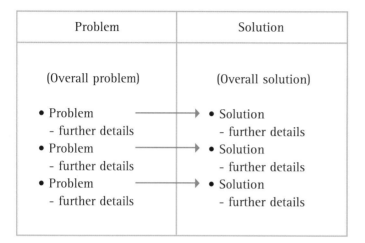

This note-taking diagram is used to show problems and their solutions. There may be many problems with many solutions or there may be one overall problem that has different solutions. In this book, there will only be a few problems with up to a couple of solutions each.

Units 4 and 10
Categorizing Diagram

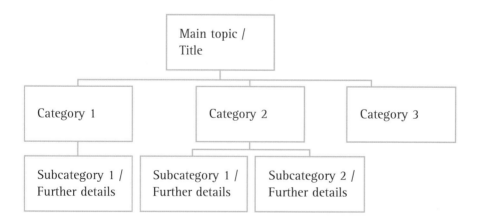

This note-taking diagram is used to show problems and their solutions. There may be many problems with many solutions or there may be one overall problem that is experienced by many things and therefore has different solutions. In this book, there will only be a few problems with up to a couple of solutions each.

Units 5 and 11
Ordering Diagram

Main Topic / Title

Step 1 Further details	→	Step 2 Further details	→	Step 3 Further details

This note-taking diagram is used to show the sequence of events or steps in a process. There can be many or only a few boxes and many or only a few details about each step. In this book, there will only be a few steps with each containing only a few further details.

Units 6 and 12
Cause and Effect Diagram

Main Topic / Title

Cause Further details	→	Effect Further details
Cause Further details	→	Effect Further details
Cause Further details	→	Effect Further details
Cause Further details	→	Effect Further details

This note-taking diagram is used to show what happens when something changes or is created. Each cause and effect can be completely independent from, or related to, the one above or below it. There can be many or only a few cause and effects with many or only a few details about each. In this book, there will either be many boxes with few details, or a few boxes with many details.

Sample Listening Lesson Plan - 50 minutes

Homework Check	5 min.	• Talk about any homework questions that the students did not understand. A combination of both teacher and peer explanations should be used.
Review	5 min.	• Review the strategies discussed in the previous lesson and talk about other strategies students might have employed when they did homework.
Main Lesson	35 min.	✱ Students often find conversations easier, so they should complete it for homework. The conversations and lectures could also be alternately taught in the classroom. **Lecture - Getting Ready to Listen** **A. Learn the words** • Preview the vocabulary and have students read the words aloud. • Talk about what parts of speech of the words belong to. ✱ Vocabulary preview can also be done immediately before the first lecture. **B. Learn the question type** • Discuss how the wording of the lecture version of the question type differs from the conversation version. (The strategies for the question type should have been learned at the end of the previous lesson and reviewed at the beginning) **Practice** **A. Lecture** • Ask the students to listen to the first part of the lecture and answer the first three questions either on their own or with a partner. • Talk about the main points and the organization of the passage as a class. • Do the fourth question as a class and explain why the note-taking diagram is most appropriate and how to use it. **B and C. Note-taking** • Have students draw the diagram and fill in some of the notes. Then check as a class that students have filled in the first part of the notes in the same way. • Have students listen to the rest of the lecture and fill in the rest of the notes. • Ask students to compare their notes with a classmate. • Emphasize that each student's notes may be written differently but that they should all include the same points. **D. TOEFL® Questions** • Ask students to do the questions. Then as a class or in pairs talk about the strategies they used to answer the questions. • In pairs or by themselves, ask the students to make another question using the target question type. When finished have the students ask their classmates their question. **E. TOEFL® Vocabulary Practice** • Ask students to complete the sentences and check their answers in pairs. **Test** • Students should complete the test individually. • Compare notes and discuss as a class what strategies were used. **Conversation - Getting Ready to Listen** (Next unit) **A. Learn the words** • Preview the vocabulary and have students read the words aloud • Talk about what parts of speech of the words belong to. **B. Learn the Question Type** • Introduce the TOEFL® question type. • Discuss strategies that can be applied to the question type.
Wrap-up	5 min.	• Give homework (the rest of the conversation section.) ✱ The lecture test section and check-up section can also be given as homework.

Teaching Tips

- It is strongly recommended to go thorough the target vocabulary prior to listening.

- It is a good idea to have students make their own vocabulary list on their PC or notebook. Putting the words under thematic categories (categories of subjects) would be an effective way to study the words.

- It is important to emphasize understanding of the main idea of the conversations and lectures. Students often listen without constructing the framework, which could cause problems understanding the main points later.

- It is important to emphasize understanding of the organization of the lectures. Understanding this enables students to choose the most appropriate note-taking diagram for the type of lecture.

- The first class should take time to introduce the note-taking diagrams. Then when students are asked to use the diagrams, they are familiar and, therefore, not as intimidating.

- In the beginning, note-taking practice needs to be done in class with the teacher's assistance because not many students are familiar with note-taking. Gradually, have students take notes in groups, pairs, and then individually.

- At least one lecture and the following questions should be done as an in-class activity; otherwise, students will not be able to understand the strategies and the new information.

- Timed question taking is an effective activity. Teachers can change the time limit as students' understanding increases.

- Encourage students to do timed activities even when they do their homework. It is a good idea to record the time they take to do the tests in their book and how many times they replayed the listening passages.

- Written and oral summaries of the lectures and conversations are recommended in order to help students understand the main point, the overall meaning, and the structure. It is also a useful exercise to prepare for the speaking and writing sections.

- Students can use the definitions and synonyms in the vocabulary section when they summarize or paraphrase the passages.

- Use the test at the end of each unit as a progress check by recording the scores of the tests, the time taken to complete the test, and the number of times the listening passage was replayed.

[01] Conversation

Getting Ready to Listen

A. Learn the words.

Key Vocabulary

password	a word required to view information
log in	to enter a computer system using an ID and/or password
personal information	details about a person containing personal facts

TOEFL® Vocabulary

ID	a way of knowing who someone is; short for identification
semester	a period of time during which school is in session
professor	a teacher with special knowledge
freshman	a person in the first year of something usually of college or university
privacy	personal life or information one wants to keep secret

B. Learn the question type.

TOEFL® Question Type

Main Idea

What problem does the man/woman have?

What is the conversation mainly about?

Why is the man/woman talking to the professor/librarian/etc?

- This type of question is asking what the conversation is mainly about or why the speakers are having the conversation.
- The answer should NOT include portions of the conversation.

Practice

A. Listen to the first part of the conversation and choose the correct answers.

Track 1-1

1. What is the main topic of the conversation?

(A) Having privacy on the computer

(B) Getting a computer ID

2. How does the student explain the problem?

(A) By giving an example

(B) By comparing and contrasting

Note-taking

B. Listen to the full conversation and take notes. Track 1-2

Woman - Student	Man - University Employee
• Wants an ID _____ • First semester - needs one for _____	 • Most freshman classes need an _____ • Passwords are _____ • If you want privacy then you have to have _____ • People can steal _____ • Tells woman to fill out form with ___ • Should be able to use _____

C. Choose the correct answers.

1. What are the speakers mainly discussing?

(A) Getting an ID to use the computer

(B) Getting a password to use the computer

2. Why is the student asking about why an ID is needed?

(A) She cannot think of a good user name and password.

(B) She thinks the computers should be available to anyone.

3. According to the man, how can the woman get an ID?

(A) By filling out a form   (B) By going to another office

TOEFL® Vocabulary Practice

D. Fill in the blanks with the correct words.

freshmen	privacy	semesters	ID	professor

1. _____ usually have to take a first-year English course.

2. Each year usually consists of two _____.

3. A(n) _____ is required to check out books from the library.

4. A _____ teaches students at a university.

5. There is often very little _____ in locker rooms.

Test

Listen to the conversation and take notes. **Track 1-3**

Man - Student	Woman - University Employee
• Never sent an _____ • Already has ID and password and has _____ _____ _____ _____ _____ _____ _____	• Thinks he will learn _____ _____ • Put arrow over picture to _____ • Professor will _____ _____ _____ _____ _____

Choose the correct answers. **Track 1-4**

1. What is the conversation mainly about?

(A) How to use a mouse

(B) How to send an email

(C) How a system works

(D) How attaching something works

2. What is the speaker's attitude when he says this:

(A) He is excited.

(B) He is angry.

(C) He is sad.

(D) He is happy.

3. According to the woman, why shouldn't the man send any personal information?

(A) It will confuse the computer system.

(B) His privacy will not be protected.

(C) His information will be lost.

(D) He will lose his password and ID number.

4. What can be inferred from the conversation? Place a checkmark in the correct box.

Statement	True	False
That man knew how to send an email.		
That man did not know how the email system worked.		
The teacher thought the man would learn quickly.		
That teacher thought that sending emails was easy.		

Lecture - History

Getting Ready to Listen

A. Learn the words.

Key Vocabulary

aggression	actions that are of a violent nature
opinion	a personal view on something
weapon	an object used to attack

TOEFL® Vocabulary

suspicion	the idea that someone or something wants to cause harm
nuclear	using the energy from an atomic reaction
compete	to try to be the best at something
military	army
political	having to do with the government or politics

B. Learn the question type.

TOEFL® Question Type

Main Idea

What is the main idea of the lecture?

What is the lecture mainly about?

- This type of question is asking about what the lecture is mainly about or why it is being given.
- The answer should NOT include portions of the lecture.

Practice

A. **Listen to the first part of the lecture and choose the correct answers.** `Track 1-5`

1. What is the main topic in this lecture?

   (A) Russian leaders   (B) The Cold War

2. What are the key points in this lecture?

   (A) The Cold War was a time of aggression mainly between the USSR and USA and was caused by different opinions.

   (B) The Cold War was a long, violent war between the US and USSR.

3. How does the professor describe the main topic?

   (A) By comparing and contrasting   (B) By giving examples

4. Choose the best note-taking diagram for this lecture.

   (A) Concept Defining   (B) Venn Diagram   (C) Problem and Solution
       Diagram   Diagram

Note-taking

B. **Draw the diagram chosen in question 4. Then insert the information from questions 1 and 2.**

C. **Now listen to the full lecture and complete your notes.** `Track 1-6`

D. Choose the correct answers.

1. What is the lecture mainly about?

(A) What the Cold War was

(B) The wars between the USSR and the US

2. What is the main point of the lecture?

(A) To discuss the bad actions by two countries

(B) To explain about the Cold War

3. According to the professor, how long did the Cold War last?

(A) Around 50 years   (B) Around 100 years

TOEFL® Vocabulary Practice

E. Fill in the blanks with the correct words.

military	compete	suspicions	nuclear	political

1. Many different teams _____ in a competition.

2. Nations usually have _____ about their enemies' plans.

3. A _____ needs the best weapons to win a war.

4. A _____ problem affects the government.

5. In order to be more powerful, countries often make _____ weapons.

Test

🎧 Listen to the lecture and take notes. **Track 1-7**

Cold War

Competing in:

- Military
  - made nuclear weapons
- Technology
  - didn't want to fall behind
- Space Race
  - wanted to be the first into space

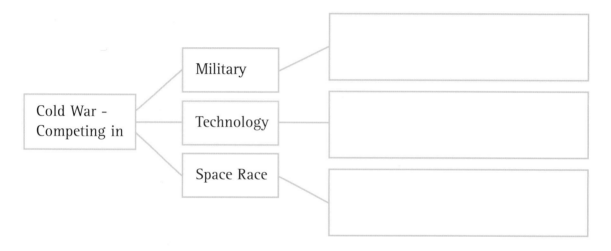

Choose the correct answers. **Track 1-8**

1. What is the lecture mainly about?

(A) The growth of the US and the USSR militaries in the Cold War

(B) The technology competition of the last fifty years

(C) The race to put people in space

(D) The ways the US and the USSR were competing in the Cold War

2. What was the space race?

(A) A race to put the first man into space

(B) A race to make the first space ship

(C) A race to be the first to land on the moon

(D) A race to create bigger and better weapons

3. What is the speaker's attitude when he says this: 🎧

    (A) He feels that they had problems.
    (B) He thinks that they were too competitive.
    (C) He believes that they were not very smart.
    (D) He thinks that they should have done more.

4. Why does the student mention the space race?

    (A) She feels that space is more interesting.
    (B) She wants to know who won.
    (C) She wants to find out about its role in the Cold War.
    (D) She is surprised that the speaker has not mentioned it.

5. How are the points in the lecture organized?

    (A) In the order that the events took place
    (B) From most complex to least complex
    (C) In the order that the textbook mentions them
    (D) From most dangerous to least dangerous

6. What does the professor imply about the countries that were involved in the Cold War? Place a checkmark in the correct box.

Statement	True	False
They reduced sizes of militaries.		
They spied on each other often.		
They stole technology secrets.		
They sent people into space.		
They wanted to be more powerful in case of war.		

Check-up

A. Choose the correct answers.

1. A conversation main idea question asks

   (A) what the speaker's emotion, attitude, or opinion is
   (B) about the relationship of ideas in the conversation
   (C) what the conversation is mainly about or why the speakers are having the conversation
   (D) why the speaker has said something

2. A lecture main idea question asks

   (A) about the relationship of ideas in the lecture
   (B) what the speaker's emotion, attitude, or opinion is
   (C) why the speaker has said something
   (D) what the lecture is mainly about or why it is being given

Key Vocabulary Practice

B. Fill in the blanks with the correct words.

weapons	personal information	password	aggressive
	logging into	opinions	

1. The country with better _____ often wins the war.

2. Most university computers require a _____.

3. An ID is used when _____ an email account.

4. An ID and password protect _____ from being seen by other people.

5. When an animal is threatened, it will often become _____.

6. The US and Soviet Union has very different _____ on which country is the best.

[02] Conversation

Getting Ready to Listen

A. Learn the words.

Key Vocabulary

course	a program of study, as in a college or university
online	accessible through a computer network, such as the Internet
computer lab	a place where many computers are kept for the use of studying

TOEFL® Vocabulary

chemistry	the study of substances
email	electronic mail sent and received through computers
revise	to reconsider and change or alter
update	to supply recent information
campus	the land and buildings that make up a school

B. Learn the question type.

TOEFL® Question Type

Detail

According to the man/woman, what is X?

What are X?

- This type of question is asking for explicit details or facts from the conversation to be identified.
- The answer will usually be consistent with the main idea of the conversation.

Practice

A. **Listen to the first part of the conversation and choose the correct answers.**

Track 1-9

1. What is the main topic of the conversation?

   (A) Getting books for a chemistry class
   (B) The homework for a chemistry class

2. How does the woman explain the problem?

   (A) By comparing different chemistry books
   (B) By saying the professor may have changed the list

Note-taking

B. **Listen to the full conversation and take notes.** Track 1-10

Man - Student	Woman - University Employee
• Needs books _____ _____	• Professor Jenkins has _____ _____
	• Asks if he has _____
	• Professor has replaced _____ _____
	• He needs _____ _____
• The office is _____ _____	• He can find the number at _____ _____
• Knows computer lab is _____ _____	• Tells him he can _____ • The computer lab is _____

C. Choose the correct answers.

1. What is the conversation mainly about?

(A) Getting books for a chemistry class

(B) Going to a computer lab

2. According to the student, what will he have to do in order to get the list?

(A) He will have to call the professor.

(B) He will have to walk to get it.

3. According to the student, why does he choose to go to the computer lab?

(A) He knows it will be open.

(B) He is good with computers.

TOEFL® Vocabulary Practice

D. Fill in the blanks with the correct words.

| chemistry | email | campus | revise | updated |

1. _____ is much faster than sending letters.

2. A _____ professor teaches students what happens when you mix two different substances.

3. It is a good idea to make sure people are _____ if there are changes to a schedule.

4. A college _____ can be located all in one place or spread out in different areas.

5. An office will often _____ its budget when it is not making enough money.

Test

Listen to the conversation and take notes. Track 1-11

Woman - Student	Man - University Employee
• Saw bookstore's _____ _____	• Store has just got them _____
• Goes to get _____ _____	• Asks if she can _____
• Wants a _____ _____	• Used books are _____ _____

Choose the correct answers. Track 1-12

1. What are the speakers mainly discussing?

   (A) Buying a textbook for class   (B) Finding a part-time job

   (C) Passing one of her courses   (D) Deciding on which course to take

2. Which of the following concerns about the book does the student mention?

   (A) Price   (B) Color

   (C) Issue number   (D) Author

3. Why does the man mention studying?

   (A) To let her know that he took the same class

   (B) To help the student with her money

   (C) To suggest that the used book will be better

   (D) To get her to buy a new book

4. Listen to part of the conversation again. Then answer the question.

   Why does the student say this: ?

   (A) To let him know that she is interested in the job

   (B) To suggest that she will start working soon

   (C) To show that she is too busy

   (D) To stop him from talking to her about it

Lecture - Art

Getting Ready to Listen

A. Learn the words.

Key Vocabulary

plan	a way of deciding how to do something ahead of time
scene	the place or setting where something occurs or is displayed
exact	correct and specific

TOEFL® Vocabulary

precise	very specific; exact
various	different and many
purpose	the reason something is done or made
represent	to create a likeness of something
reproduce	to make again in a new way

B. Learn the question type.

TOEFL® Question Type

Detail

According to the professor, what is X?

What are X?

- This type of question is asking for explicit details or facts from the lecture to be identified.
- The answer will usually be consistent with the main idea of the lecture.

Practice

A. **Listen to the first part of the lecture and choose the correct answers.** `Track 1-13`

1. What is the main topic in this lecture?

   (A) Neo-Impressionism   (B) Georges Seurat

2. What is the key point in this lecture?

   (A) Neo-Impressionism art was the new art in the 1880s and was different from other art because of its precise style.

   (B) Only Seurat used Neo-Impressionism and no one liked it.

3. How does the professor describe the main topic?

   (A) By introducing an order   (B) By comparing and contrasting

4. Choose the best note-taking diagram for this lecture.

   (A) Venn Diagram   (B) Categorizing Diagram   (C) Ordering Diagram

Note-taking

B. **Draw the diagram chosen in question 4. Then insert the information from questions 1 and 2.**

C. **Now listen to the full lecture and complete your notes.** `Track 1-14`

D. Choose the correct answers.

1. What is the lecture mainly about?

    (A) How Neo-Impressionism was different from other art

    (B) How George Seurat was a Neo-Impressionist

2. What is Neo-Impressionism?

    (A) A style of painting that used brush strokes

    (B) A new style of painting in the 1880's

3. According to the professor, what is one way these new artists were different?

    (A) They mixed paint colors together.

    (B) They didn't mix paint colors.

TOEFL® Vocabulary Practice

E. Fill in the blanks with the correct words.

precise	various	reproduce	purpose	represent

1. _____ artists tried Seurat's way of painting.

2. The _____ of Neo-Impressionism was to create natural and realistic art.

3. Impressionist art is not _____ like Neo-Impressionist art is.

4. A piece of art can _____ many different things to many different people.

5. Impressionist artists did not try to _____ people or scenes in a life-like way.

Test

Listen to the lecture and take notes. **Track 1-15**

Seurat's Style

- Precise painting
- Planned carefully
- Used pure color
- Used dots

Seurat's Style   Older Styles

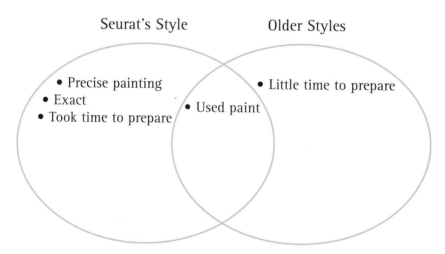

- Precise painting
- Exact
- Took time to prepare
- Used paint
- Little time to prepare

Choose the correct answers. **Track 1-16**

1. What is the lecture mainly about?

    (A) The way the eye sees colors
    (B) The steps to painting in a Neo-Impressionist style
    (C) The artists who learned from Seurat
    (D) The difference between painting styles

2. What is the professor's opinion of this style of painting?

    (A) He thinks painting in brush strokes is a better way.
    (B) He is surprised that so many artists are good at it.
    (C) He thinks it is difficult to learn.
    (D) He doesn't like it.

3. According to the professor, why did Seurat not blend his paints?

    (A) He thought it would ruin the paints.

    (B) He thought mixed paints did not look real.

    (C) He thought blended paints made paintings look too divided.

    (D) He thought it would make the art bright.

4. Why does the professor say this: 🎧 ?

    (A) To explain to students how much time it takes to allow the dots to dry

    (B) To emphasize how much time it took Seurat to paint a picture

    (C) To tell students that this artwork lasts forever

    (D) To help students understand how old this painting style is

5. How did the professor organize the information about this way of painting?

    (A) By describing only Seurat's style

    (B) By describing only other styles

    (C) By comparing Seurat and other Neo-Impressionists

    (D) By comparing Neo-Impressionism and other styles

6. Based on the information in the lecture, indicate whether the author mentions the following statements about the Seurat's method of painting. For each sentence, put a checkmark in the True or False column.

Statement	True	False
Takes a very long time to complete.		
Colors must be blended well.		
Tiny dots are used instead of strokes.		
Must plan well before painting.		

Check-up

A. Choose the correct answers.

1. A conversation detail question asks

   (A) for explicit details or facts from the conversation to be identified
   (B) about the relationship of ideas in a conversation
   (C) what the conversation is about
   (D) why the speaker has said something

2. A lecture detail question asks

   (A) about the overall organization of the lecture
   (B) what the lecture is about
   (C) for explicit details or facts from the lecture to be identified
   (D) what the speaker's emotion, attitude, or opinion is

Key Vocabulary Practice

B. Fill in the blanks with the correct words.

| courses | online | computer lab | plan | scenes | exact |

1. Students often work in a _____ at school.

2. It is a good idea to have a _____ when building a house.

3. The _____ definition of a word can be found in a dictionary.

4. Students in university take many _____ every year.

5. It is easy to find information quickly _____.

6. Seurat often included people and nature in his _____.

[03] Conversation

Getting Ready to Listen

A. Learn the words.

Key Vocabulary

essay	a short piece of writing on a particular subject or theme
lesson	a class period in which something is learned or studied
introduction	the part at the beginning of something that explains what is to follow

TOEFL® Vocabulary

format	a layout or design
paragraph	a portion of writing that deals with a specific idea
evidence	something that helps to support an idea
organization	the logical arrangement of something
summary	a short report that highlights main ideas and points

B. Learn the question type.

TOEFL® Question Type

Function

What does the man/woman imply when he/she says this: ◯ ?
What does the man/woman mean when he/she says this: ◯ ?
Why does the man/woman say this: ◯ ?

You will hear part of the conversation again.

- This type of question is asking why the speaker has said something; it may not match what he/she directly states.
- To get the correct answer, tone of voice, stress on a certain work or phrase, or intonation should be paid attention to.

Practice

A. Listen to the first part of the conversation and choose the correct answers.
Track 1-17

1. What is the main topic in this conversation?

(A) How to get a better grade in class

(B) How to write a better essay

2. How does the student explain the problem?

(A) By describing what he understands

(B) By describing his essay

Note-taking

B. Listen to the full conversation and take notes. Track 1-18

Man - Student	Woman - Professor

• Asks how to write a _____ _____
 	
 • Takes many notes and _____ _____ _____
	• Tells the student that a good essay needs _____
	 • Goes over the _____
	 • Three _____
	     1. _____
	       - gives the main idea
	     2. Body _____
	       - provides _____ _____
	     3. Conclusion
	       - is _____
	 • Tells the student that good _____ _____

C. Choose the correct answers.

1. According to the woman, what are the three parts in an essay?

(A) Introduction, body paragraphs, and a conclusion

(B) Organization, notes, and a main idea

2. What does the student mean when he says this: ( ) ? `Track 1-19`

(A) He thinks he is doing everything he should be doing.

(B) He thinks the class is too easy.

3. Why did the student say this: ( ) ? `Track 1-20`

(A) To admit that he hadn't tried very hard before

(B) To show that he is learning something new

TOEFL® Vocabulary Practice

D. Fill in the blanks with the correct words.

format	paragraph	evidence	organization	summary

1. An essay can be improved by following a simple _____.

2. A body _____ of an essay focuses on evidence for the main idea.

3. When researching something, it's a good idea to make a _____ of the information.

4. A writer must always provide enough _____ to support his arguments.

5. The _____ of ideas is important before beginning to write an essay.

Test

🎧 **Listen to the conversation and take notes.** `Track 1-21`

Woman - Student	Man - Professor
• Needs help with _____ • Is having problems _____ _____ • Not good _____ _____ _____ _____ _____ _____ _____	• Talks about finding _____ _____ • Books are _____ • Can look _____ • Internet - _____ _____ • Books - _____ _____ _____ _____ _____

Choose the correct answers. `Track 1-22`

1. What is the conversation mainly about?

(A) Giving a presentation
(B) Organizing an essay in a clear way
(C) Finding a partner for a class project
(D) Finding information and taking notes

2. What does the professor recommend doing when taking notes?

(A) Writing as quickly as possible   (B) Making a summary
(C) Checking the information   (D) Getting lots of information

3. Why does the professor say this: 🎧 ?

(A) To suggest that she only needs to read the summary
(B) To explain how to search for information
(C) To bring an end to the conversation
(D) To emphasize that only the main points should be copied down

4. What is the likely outcome of using both books and computers as sources?

(A) The student will need help doing the research.
(B) The student will not be able to finish her project.
(C) The student will have plenty of information.
(D) The student will like books more than the computer.

Lecture - Zoology

Getting Ready to Listen

A. Learn the words.

Key Vocabulary

deep sleep	a sound and heavy sleep
disappear	to stop being seen or to stop existing
underground	below the surface of the ground

TOEFL® Vocabulary

creature	a living thing, usually an animal
solve	to find the answer to, or explanation for, something
sensitive	easily affected by something
average	usual; ordinary
shield	to protect or defend from something

B. Learn the question type.

TOEFL® Question Type

Function

What does the professor imply when he/she says this: 🎧 ?

What does the professor mean when he/she says this: 🎧 ?

Why does the professor say this: 🎧 ?

You will hear part of the lecture again.

- This type of question is asking why the speaker has said something; it may not match what he/she directly states.
- To get the correct answer tone of voice, stress on a certain work or phrase or intonation should be paid attention to.

Practice

A. Listen to the first part of the lecture and choose the correct answers. `Track 1-23`

1. What is the main topic of this lecture?

   (A) Different animals that hibernate

   (B) Bats in winter

2. What are the key points in this lecture?

   (A) The winter is a bad time of year for animals and they all sleep.

   (B) Bats hibernate because it is cold and it is hard to find food in winter

3. How does the professor describe the main topic?

   (A) By putting steps in order   (B) By giving problems and solutions

4. Choose the best note-taking diagram for this lecture.

   (A) Problem and Solution   (B) Venn Diagram   (C) Concept Defining Diagram
   Diagram

Note-taking

B. Draw the diagram chosen in question 4. Then insert the information from questions 1 and 2. `Track 1-24`

C. Now listen to the full lecture and complete your notes.

D. Choose the correct answers.

1. What is hibernation?

(A) A deep sleep   (B) An extreme cold

2. Why does the professor say this: 🎧 ? `Track 1-25`

(A) To ask for the students' participation

(B) To emphasize her point about the bats' food

3. What does the professor imply when she says this: 🎧 ? `Track 1-26`

(A) Bats stop hibernating in the spring

(B) Bats live off their fat during the spring.

TOEFL® Vocabulary Practice

E. Fill in the blanks with the correct words.

sensitive	creature	shield	average	solving

1. A bat is a _____ that hibernates.

2. Sunscreen is used to _____ people from the sun's dangerous rays.

3. The _____ person needs eight hours of sleep a night.

4. Most animals that live underground are very _____ to sunlight.

5. Math homework usually involves _____ a lot of different problems.

Test

🎧 Listen to the lecture and take notes. `Track 1-27`

How snakes protect themselves

- Rattlesnake
  - small beads

- Spitting Cobra
  - sprays poison

- Hognose snake
  - plays dead

How Snakes Protect Themselves

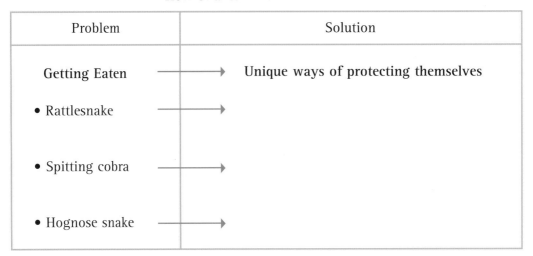

Problem	Solution
Getting Eaten ⟶	Unique ways of protecting themselves
• Rattlesnake ⟶	
• Spitting cobra ⟶	
• Hognose snake ⟶	

Choose the correct answers. `Track 1-28`

1. What is the lecture about?

(A) The feeding habits of snakes
(B) How certain snakes protect themselves
(C) The most dangerous snakes in the world
(D) The different uses of snake poison

2. Why does the professor discuss the beads on a rattlesnake's tail

(A) To show how the snake is more dangerous than other snakes
(B) To compare the snake to less scary animals
(C) To explain how the snake scares off animals
(D) To describe how the snake uses its tail to hunt

3. According to the professor, where does the spitting cobra spray its poison?

(A) At the animal it is hunting

(B) At other snakes

(C) At the tongue of an animal that is attacking it

(D) At the eyes of an animal that is attacking it

4. Why does the professor say this: ⌒ ?

(A) To emphasize that the snake sprays its poison at a specific place

(B) To explain how the snake must be careful not to spray itself

(C) To show how the snake has very little poison

(D) To describe how much poison the snake makes

5. What is the professor's attitude towards the hognose snake?

(A) She is amazed by it.

(B) She thinks that it is stupid.

(C) She thinks that it is the best snake.

(D) She thinks that it is the most dangerous.

6. Indicate whether each of the following is mentioned in the lecture.

Statement	True	False
The rattlesnake rattles its tail.		
The spitting cobra sprays poison at the eyes of its attacker.		
The hognose snake pretends to be sick.		
Beads in a rattlesnake's tail make the sound.		
There are no creatures that eat snakes.		

Check-up

A. **Choose the correct answers.**

1. A conversation function question asks

   (A) what the speaker's emotion, attitude, or opinion is
   (B) for explicit details or facts from the conversation to be identified
   (C) why the speaker has said something
   (D) about the relationship of ideas in the conversation

2. A lecture function question asks

   (A) why the speaker has said something
   (B) what the lecture is about
   (C) for explicit details or facts from the lecture to be identified
   (D) what the speaker's emotion, attitude, or opinion is

Key Vocabulary Practice

B. **Fill in the blanks with the correct words.**

introduction	essay	lessons	deep sleep
	disappear	underground	

1. A bat will go into a _____ during the winter in order to survive.

2. The _____ of an essay is at the beginning.

3. Many animals and insects live _____ during the winter.

4. An introduction, body paragraphs, and conclusion make up an _____.

5. Students must attend all _____ to learn all the information.

6. It seems like many animals _____ in winter, but they are just hibernating.

[04] Conversation

Getting Ready to Listen

A. Learn the words.

Key Vocabulary

check out	to fulfill all requirements in taking away something
self-service	serving oneself, without the help of another person
press	to push against

TOEFL® Vocabulary

research	the collecting of information to find out facts and points about a subject
scan	to move a beam of light over a surface in order to capture an image digitally
account	a business relationship that provides services
receipt	a printed note, usually given after some sort of transaction
due	the time something should be returned

B. Learn the question type.

TOEFL® Question Type

Attitude

What is the man/woman's attitude towards X?

What is the man/woman's opinion of X?

- This type of question is asking what the speaker's emotion, attitude, or opinion is; it may not match what he/she directly states.
- To get the correct answer, tone of voice, stress on a certain word or phrase, or intonation should be paid attention to.
- Some questions will replay part of the conversation again.

Practice

A. Listen to the first part of the conversation and choose the correct answers.

Track 1-29

1. What is the main topic of this conversation?

   (A) The different sections of the library

   (B) How to check out library books

2. How does the man explain the solution?

   (A) By mentioning the ways to check out books

   (B) By describing which books to check out

Note-taking

B. Listen to the full conversation and take notes. Track 1-30

Woman - Student	Man - Librarian
• Needs help to _____ _____ • Has to do _____ _____ • Has a student library _____ _____	• Two choices: 　　1. use the _____ 　　2. go to _____ • Self-service machine: 　　- looks like _____ 　　- scan _____ 　　- then _____ 　　- machine will print _____ 　　_____ 　　- press ID and books because _____ 　　_____ • Take books to _____ 　　- librarian will _____

C. Choose the correct answers.

Listen again to part of the conversation. Then answer the question. 🎧 `Track 1-31`

1. What is the student's attitude towards the instructions?

    (A) She is still unsure about how to check out books.

    (B) She is more interested in one of the methods.

2. What is the student's opinion of the checkout process?

    (A) She thinks that the library needs to update its methods.

    (B) She thinks it will not be too hard to check out books.

3. Why does the student say this: 🎧 ? `Track 1-32`

    (A) To remind the man to tell her about the other option

    (B) To show the man she is angry

TOEFL® Vocabulary Practice

D. Fill in the blanks with the correct words.

research	account	scan	receipt	due

1. Homework is often assigned with a _____ date.

2. The information on a _____ often shows what was purchased and how much it cost.

3. It is necessary to do a lot of _____ when writing an essay on a new topic.

4. Supermarket self-service machines require the customer to _____ their own groceries.

5. A bank _____ allows people to store their money safely.

Test

Listen to the conversation and take notes. Track 1-33

Man - Student	Woman - Librarian
• Is doing research for _____ _____ • Doesn't know where _____ _____ _____ _____ _____ _____ _____ _____ _____ _____	• There are two ways: 1. Computer _____ 2. Book _____ • Book lists: _____ _____ _____ _____ _____ _____ _____

Choose the correct answers. Track 1-34

1. Why is the student looking for help?

(A) He is supposed to meet with one of his friends.

(B) He is looking for a part-time job.

(C) He wants to know how to find a book.

(D) He is struggling with his job.

2. How does the woman organize the instructions for finding a book in the library?

(A) By explaining the easiest option then the most difficult option

(B) By explaining how to check out

(C) By explaining the most difficult option then the easiest option

(D) By explaining only one option

3. How does the book listing organize the books?

(A) Alphabetically

(B) By the author's name

(C) By the subject and then title

(D) By the subject and then the author's name

4. What is implied about the student's opinion of finding a book?

(A) He thinks it will be easier than he expected.

(B) He doesn't think that he can do it.

(C) He is not looking forward to trying to find a book.

(D) He thinks that the librarian should find it for him.

Lecture - Physics

Getting Ready to Listen

A. Learn the words.

Key Vocabulary

ray	a narrow beam of light
bounce	to hit a surface and rebound away from it quickly with a lot of energy
direction	the path a person or object moves along

TOEFL® Vocabulary

lecture	a talk about a subject given to a group or class
property	an important quality
repeat	to do again
remember	to recall something from memory
material	a solid substance

B. Learn the question type.

TOEFL® Question Type

Attitude

What is the professor's attitude towards X?

What is the professor's opinion of X?

- This type of question is asking what the speaker's emotion, attitude, or opinion is; it may not match what he/she directly states.
- To get the correct answer, tone of voice, stress on a certain work or phrase, or intonation should be paid attention to.
- Some questions will replay part of the lecture again.

Practice

A. Listen to the first part of the lecture and choose the correct answers. `Track 1-35`

1. What is the main topic of the lecture?
    (A) Properties of light   (B) What light is

2. What are the key points in this lecture?
    (A) Reflection and refraction are two types of repeated light.
    (B) Reflection and refraction are two main properties of light.

3. How does the professor describe the main topic?
    (A) By dividing it into two categories
    (B) By explaining its cause and effects

4. Choose the best note-taking diagram for this lecture.
    (A) Ordering Diagram   (B) Concept Defining   (C) Categorizing Diagram
                           Diagram

Note-taking

B. Draw the diagram chosen in question 4. Then insert the information from questions 1 and 2.

C. Now listen to the full lecture and complete your notes. `Track 1-36`

D. Choose the correct answers.

1. What is the professor's opinion of reflection?

    (A) It is not difficult to learn about.

    (B) It is similar to refraction.

2. What does the professor imply when she says this: 🎧 ? **Track 1-37**

    (A) That she is sure that the students know what light is

    (B) That she is unsure if the students know what light is

3. What does the professor imply when she says this: 🎧 ? **Track 1-38**

    (A) She thinks that the example will help the students understand.

    (B) She thinks the students disagree with her.

TOEFL® Vocabulary Practice

E. Fill in the blanks with the correct words.

lecture	repeat	remember	materials	property

1. A _____ is often taught to hundreds of students.

2. Students who fail their final exams often have to _____ the course.

3. Physics often uses long mathematical formulas that can be difficult to

    _____.

4. A _____ of gravity is that things are pulled to the ground.

5. Building a house requires many different _____.

Listen to the lecture and take notes. Track 1-39

Heat Transfer

- **Convection**
  - heat moves through gases and liquids

- **Conduction**
  - heat moves through solids

- **Radiation**
  - can feel heat without touching

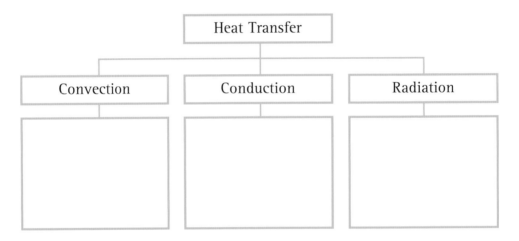

Choose the correct answers. Track 1-40

1. What is the lecture mainly about?

   (A) What heat is
   (B) How heat transfers
   (C) The properties of heat
   (D) Heat in hot air balloons

2. What happens to a hot air balloon because of convection?

   (A) The balloon's air is heated
   (B) The balloon becomes filled with gas
   (C) The balloon goes up and goes down
   (D) The balloon's flame gets hotter and hotter

3. What is the professor's opinion of conduction?

   (A) He finds it easiest to teach by cooking.
   (B) He feels that it is good for making buildings.
   (C) He believes that it is useful heating buildings.
   (D) He thinks many people get hurt from it.

4. Why does the professor mention a toaster?

   (A) To explain how toast is made by convection
   (B) To discuss how conduction makes toasters hot
   (C) To give an example of something that burns people
   (D) To give an example of heat radiation

5. Why does the professor say this: ◯ ?

   (A) To find out how many students have been near a fire
   (B) To give students an example of radiation
   (C) To show how dangerous fire is
   (D) To get students to try this

6. Based on the information in the lecture, indicate whether the professor mentions the following statements about heat transfer. For each sentence, put a checkmark in the True or False column.

Statement	True	False
Heat moving through liquid or gas is convection.		
Convection is a pattern that repeats.		
Heat cannot move through solid materials.		
Some materials are better at conducting heat than others.		
Radiating heat cannot be seen.		

Check-up

A. Choose the correct answers.

1. A conversation attitude question asks

(A) why the speaker has said something
(B) what the speaker's emotion, attitude, or opinion is
(C) about the relationship of ideas in the conversation
(D) what the conversation is about

2. A lecture attitude question asks

(A) about the relationship of ideas in the lecture
(B) what the lecture is about
(C) why the speaker has said something
(D) what the speaker's emotion, attitude, or opinion is

Key Vocabulary Practice

B. Fill in the blanks with the correct words.

pressed	self-service	check out	bounce	directions	ray

1. In a _____ restaurant the customers get their own food.

2. In order to turn a computer on, a button must be _____.

3. In order to _____ a book from the library, the person must have an ID.

4. Light rays are reflected in different _____ when they hit the surface of water.

5. Basketball players _____ a ball on the court.

6. Sometimes when the clouds part, a _____ of sunlight can appear.

[05] Conversation

Getting Ready to Listen

A. Learn the words.

Key Vocabulary

mathematics	the study of numbers, sums, and shapes
cheat	to act dishonestly
punish	to penalize someone for doing wrong

TOEFL® Vocabulary

tutor	to teach privately
major	a chosen field of study
clarify	to make clear
standard	normal; usual
strategy	a plan of action for managing situations and problems

B. Learn the question type.

TOEFL® Question Type

Organization

How did the man/woman organize the information about X?

How is the discussion organized?

Why does the man/woman discuss X?

- This type of question is asking about the overall organization of the conversation or the relationship between two parts of the conversation.
- The answer may take into account what examples have been given or look at comparisons that have been made.

Practice

Track 1-41

A. Listen to the first part of the conversation and choose the correct answers.

1. What is the main topic in this conversation?

   (A) Taking a math test
   (B) Getting a tutor

2. How does the woman explain the problem?

   (A) By saying there are some things she can and cannot do
   (B) By saying that she will help

Note-taking

B. Listen to the full conversation and take notes. Track 1-42

Man - Student	Woman - Tutor
• Asks if the woman is _____ _____ • Needs help with _____ _____	• Tells the man she _____ • Is a _____ • Can help but _____ _____ • Some things she can _____ _____ • Rules against _____ _____
• Doesn't want either _____ _____	• If cheat then _____ • Can help with learning strategies, ____ _____ _____
• Thinks _____	• With class work and _____ _____

C. Choose the correct answers.

1. Why does the tutor mention her major?

(A) To suggest that he needs another tutor

(B) To prove that she can help the student

2. How does the tutor explain the rules?

(A) By giving a history of how the rules have been used at the school

(B) By explaining what could happen if they break the rules

3. What is the student's attitude towards hearing there are rules?

(A) He is surprised.   (B) He is happy.

TOEFL® Vocabulary Practice

D. Fill in the blanks with the correct words.

major	tutor	standard	strategies	clarify

1. Most governments have specific _____ to deal with terrorists.

2. A mathematics _____ studies numbers, sums, or shapes.

3. Teachers often use interesting examples to _____ the points of their lessons.

4. If a student needs extra help in a subject, they usually get someone to _____ them.

5. A dress code is _____ in most schools.

Test

Listen to the conversation and take notes. **Track 1-43**

Woman - Student	Man - Tutor
• Having problems in _____ _____	
• Doesn't understand professor's _____ _____ _____ _____ _____ _____ _____ _____ _____	• Decides on some _____ _____ _____ _____ _____ _____ _____ _____ _____ _____

Choose the correct answers. **Track 1-44**

1. What is the conversation mainly about?

    (A) A student who is trying to find a tutor
    (B) A student who has problems with tests
    (C) A student who has problems with their homework
    (D) A student who is having trouble finding a partner to work with

2. According to the tutor, what does more math work do?

    (A) Helps the student understand the professor's notes
    (B) Bores the student
    (C) Makes the student quicker at math problems
    (D) Helps the student understand the work

3. Listen again to part of the conversation. Then answer the question.

    Why does the man say this: ?
    (A) To suggest that he might be wrong (B) To explain his point better
    (C) To make the student feel bad   (D) To give the student the answer

4. Why does the tutor mention getting paid?

    (A) To show that he makes a lot of money
    (B) To show how much money he gets paid
    (C) To show that he wants more money
    (D) To show that she is wasting her money by not preparing

Lecture - Business

Getting Ready to Listen

A. Learn the words.

Key Vocabulary

billboard	an outdoor board, on which advertisements are displayed
couple	a few; two
support	to help prove; to help or aid a purpose

TOEFL® Vocabulary

promote	to help the growth, success, or development of something
attract	to catch the interest of someone
attention	a general focused interest that leads people to want to know more
process	a method or way of doing something that involves a series of steps
focus	the center of interest or activity

B. Learn the question type.

TOEFL® Question Type

Organization

How did the professor organize the information about X?

How is the discussion organized?

Why does the professor discuss X?

- This type of question is asking about the overall organization of the lecture or the relationship between two parts of the lecture.
- The answer will take into account what examples have been given or look at comparisons that have been made.

Practice

A. **Listen to the first part of the lecture and choose the correct answers.** `Track 1-45`

1. What is the main topic in this lecture?

   (A) Advertising   (B) Billboard advertising

2. What are the key points in this lecture?

   (A) Advertisers must know the product, then choose the ad's focus, and then its picture.
   (B) Advertisers must choose the right product then choose the advertisement.

3. How does the professor describe the main topic?

   (A) By categorizing types of advertisements
   (B) By putting the steps in order

4. Choose the best note-taking diagram for this lecture.

   (A) Problem and Solution   (B) Venn Diagram   (C) Ordering Diagram
        Diagram

Note-taking

B. **Draw the diagram chosen in question 4. Then insert the information from questions 1 and 2.**

C. **Now listen to the full lecture and complete your notes.** `Track 1-46`

D. Choose the correct answers.

1. How does the professor organize the lecture?

(A) He categorizes the different types of advertisements.

(B) He lists the steps it takes to create a billboard.

2. Why does the professor mention the milk billboard?

(A) To give an example

(B) To use the advertisement to discuss its problems

3. What is the professor's opinion of billboard advertising?

(A) He thinks billboard advertising is very bad.

(B) He thinks billboard advertising is useful.

TOEFL® Vocabulary Practice

E. Fill in the blanks with the correct words.

promoting	attract	attention	process	focus

1. The goal of any advertisement is to _____ customers.

2. The _____ of an advertisement must be clear so people know what the product is.

3. _____ a concert will increase the chance of people coming.

4. Choosing a picture for an advertisement is the final step in the _____.

5. A good advertisement grabs the customer's _____.

Test

🎧 Listen to the lecture and take notes. `Track 1-47`

The Four P's

- Product
  - Make a product to sell
- Price
  - Decide on a price
- Place
  - Find a place to sell
- Promotion
  - Advertising

The Four P's

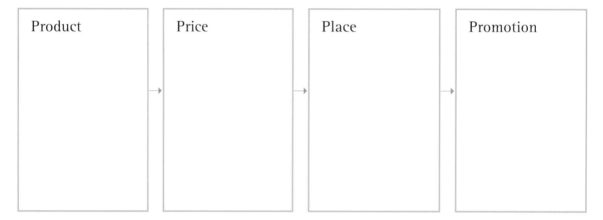

Product	Price	Place	Promotion

Choose the correct answers. `Track 1-48`

1. What is the lecture mainly about?

(A) How to buy a product

(B) How to sell a product

(C) Designing computer games

(D) The importance of advertising

2. Why does the professor mention computer games?

  (A) To show how good they are
  (B) To compare it to other products
  (C) To show how to use the Four P's
  (D) To get students to buy them

3. According to the professor, what is promotion?

  (A) It is often advertising.
  (B) It is the second last step in the Four P's process.
  (C) It is the most important part.
  (D) It is only found on TV.

Listen again to part of the lecture. Then answer the question. ◯

4. Why does the professor say this: ◯ ?

  (A) To ask the students if they would buy computer games
  (B) To ask the students where they think it should be sold
  (C) To emphasize the importance of stores
  (D) To tell the student where they should be sold

5. What is the professor's opinion of computer games?

  (A) She does not think that the students should play them.
  (B) She thinks they make a good example.
  (C) She thinks that she can sell them better.
  (D) She does not think that they are popular.

6. What can be inferred about the promotion of a product?

  (A) Its main goal is to attract attention.
  (B) It is the most important step of the "Four P's."
  (C) It is best when done online.
  (D) It isn't very important.

Check-up

A. Choose the correct answers.

1. A conversation organization question asks

   (A) for explicit details or facts from the conversation to be identified
   (B) what the speaker's emotion, attitude, or opinion is
   (C) about the organization of, or the relationship between two parts of, the conversation
   (D) what the conversation is about or why the speakers are having the conversation

2. A lecture organization question asks

   (A) about the organization of, or the relationship between two parts of, the lecture
   (B) what the lecture is about or why it is being given
   (C) for explicit details or facts from the lecture to be identified
   (D) about the relationship of ideas in a passage

Key Vocabulary Practice

B. Fill in the blanks with the correct words.

billboard	couple	punished	cheats
	mathematics	support	

1. When a student _____ they are sometimes told to leave school.

2. Students often study _____ all throughout their grade school years.

3. If someone cheats during a test they are usually _____.

4. Only a _____ of stores sell foreign computer games.

5. The picture on an advertisement has to _____ what is being promoted.

6. A _____ is a great place to put an ad because it can be seen by many people.

[06] Conversation

Getting Ready to Listen

A. Learn the words.

Key Vocabulary

absent	not present; missing
classmate	a member of the same class at school
outline	a plan or report that describes only the main points

TOEFL® Vocabulary

project	an organized activity undertaken by a student or a group of students
extension	a period of extra time
grade	a mark or score in a school course of study
scholarship	money that is given to help pay the cost of school
tuition	the amount it costs to attend a school

B. Learn the question type.

TOEFL® Question Type

Content

What is the likely outcome of doing X then Y?

What can be inferred about X?

Indicate whether each of the following was mentioned in the conversation.

• This type of question is asking about the relationship of ideas in the conversation.

• The answer may include ideas that have been stated or implied.

• The question may include a table for information to be organized into.

Practice

A. Listen to the first part of the conversation and choose the correct answers.
Track 1-49

1. What is the main topic of this conversation?

    (A) Ways a student can make up for missed lectures
    (B) How to avoid getting sick and missing school

2. How does the student explain the problem?

    (A) By going over the cause of the sickness
    (B) By explaining what she missed

Note-taking

B. Listen to the full conversation and take notes. Track 1-50

Woman - Student	Man - Professor
• Wants an _____ • Has been _____ _____ • Needs a good grade or _____ _____	• Can't _____ • Can suggest _____ _____ • Tells her to borrow _____ _____ _____ • Or go to the library and _____ _____ • He can give an _____ _____ • She can look up _____ _____ • Thinks she will be _____

C. Choose the correct answers.

1. Why does the professor mention outlines?

(A) To show how he could help the student

(B) To explain what the student should do

2. What is the likely outcome of the student borrowing notes and doing more research?

(A) She will not understand the material.

(B) She will have enough information to finish the project.

3. Indicate whether each of the following was mentioned in the conversation. Place a checkmark in the correct box.

Statement	True	False
The professor gave the student an extension.		
The student could lose her scholarship.		
The student cannot borrow notes.		

TOEFL® Vocabulary Practice

D. Fill in the blanks with the correct words.

projects	extension	grades	scholarship	tuition

1. A private school usually has high _____ fees.

2. Someone who is a very good student might get a _____.

3. Teachers often use group _____ to help students learn how to work together.

4. If a student has been sick, then he or she might be given an _____ on due dates.

5. Scholarships are often given to students with good _____.

Test

Listen to the conversation and take notes. Track 1-51

Man - Student	Woman - Professor
• Has a problem with _____ _____	• She _____
• Isn't doing work and _____ _____	• Is happy with _____ _____
• Is going to need _____ _____ _____ _____ _____ _____ _____ _____ _____ _____	• Two choices: _____ _____ _____ _____ _____ _____ _____

Choose the correct answers. Track 1-52

1. What problem does the student have?

(A) He has been sick. (B) He would like to get an extension.

(C) He is going to miss some lectures. (D) He has a partner who isn't doing his work.

2. According to the student, what is important to him?

(A) He needs a better partner. (B) He needs to get good grades.

(C) He needs an extension. (D) He needs more scholarships.

3. What is the professor's opinion of the partner?

(A) She thinks that the partner is not working hard enough.

(B) She thinks the partner is a good student.

(C) She thinks that the partner should be left alone.

(D) She feels that the partner is working very hard.

4. What information is true of the student, and what is true of the professor?
For each phrase below, place a checkmark in the correct box.

	Student	Professor
Is not going to make the deadline		
Offers to talk to the partner		
Is happy with the tutoring work		
Thinks of two possible solutions		

Lecture - Astronomy

Getting Ready to Listen

A. Learn the words.

Key Vocabulary

Earth	the planet that we live on
cosmic	involving the universe or space
space	the area that contains all things in the universe

TOEFL® Vocabulary

temperature	the degree of heat or cold in a body or an environment
cause	a person or thing that brings about an action or a result
proof	evidence that something is true
affect	to cause a change in or have an effect on something
particle	a very small piece or part

B. Learn the question type.

TOEFL® Question Type

Content

What is the likely outcome/was the outcome of doing X then Y?

What can be inferred about X?

Indicate whether each of the following was mentioned in the lecture.

- This type of question is asking about the relationship of ideas in the lecture.
- The answer may include ideas that have been stated or implied.
- The question may include a table for information to be organized into.

Practice

Track 1-53

A. Listen to the first part of the lecture and choose the correct answers.

1. What is the main topic in this lecture?

   (A) Cosmic rays   (B) Pollution

2. What are the key points in this lecture?

   (A) Cosmic rays affect the Earth's temperatures
   (B) Cosmic rays are affected by pollution

3. How does the professor describe the main topic?

   (A) By comparing cosmic rays to clouds
   (B) By describing the effects of cosmic rays

4. Choose the best note-taking diagram for this lecture.

   (A) Problem and Solution   (B) Venn Diagram   (C) Cause and Effect
       Diagram   Diagram

Note-taking

B. Draw the diagram chosen in question 4. Then insert the information from questions 1 and 2.

Track 1-54

C. Now listen to the full lecture and complete your notes.

D. Choose the correct answers.

1. What is the likely outcome of fewer cosmic rays hitting the Earth?

    (A) The Earth will become cooler.

    (B) Fewer clouds will form.

2. What will happen if fewer cosmic rays continue to reach the Earth?

    (A) The Earth's temperature will continue rise.

    (B) The Earth's temperatures will go down.

3. Why does the professor mention pollution?

    (A) To show another reason for a rise in temperatures

    (B) To show that cosmic rays are not the cause of the rise in temperature

TOEFL® Vocabulary Practice

E. Fill in the blanks with the correct words.

temperature	cause	proof	affected	particles

1. Global Warming is causing the Earth's _____ to rise.

2. Scientists must have _____ of something before it becomes a fact.

3. The Earth's temperature is _____ by the sun.

4. The sun's cosmic rays break into tiny _____ when they hit the Earth.

5. One _____ of global warming may be pollution.

Test

Listen to the lecture and take notes. `Track 1-55`

Space Junk

- Small particles
- Becomes dangerous
- Orbits the Earth
- Floats in space

Space Junk

Cause		Effect
Small particles of metal	→	Becomes dangerous space junk
Junk such as paint	→	Made a dent on
	→	
	→	

Choose the correct answers. `Track 1-56`

1. What is the lecture mainly about?

(A) How to clean up space junk
(B) The effects space junk has on shuttles
(C) How to identify the types of space junk
(D) Why space shuttles are painted

2. According to the professor, why is space junk dangerous?

    (A) It can fall to the Earth.
    (B) It moves at a very high speed.
    (C) It can become too cold.
    (D) It can become too hot.

Listen again to part of the lecture. Then answer the question. ◯

3. Why does the professor say this: ◯ ?

    (A) Because the student does not believe him
    (B) Because the student already knows the answer
    (C) Because he is upset with the student for interrupting
    (D) Because he is almost finished with the lecture

4. Why does the professor mention how a recent space shuttle got dented?

    (A) To show how space junk can only do small amounts of damage
    (B) To prove that space shuttles use strong metals to protect them
    (C) To explain how pieces of paint are the most dangerous junk
    (D) To give an example of the damage that space junk can cause

Listen again to part of the lecture. Then answer the question. ◯

5. What is the professor's attitude towards how shuttles orbit?

    (A) He believes that it will cause more problems.
    (B) He is impressed at the solution to the problem.
    (C) He thinks it is a strange way to move a space shuttle.
    (D) He feels the shuttle pilots are clever.

6. What can be inferred about what a larger piece of space junk would do if it hit a shuttle?

    (A) The shuttle might be fine.
    (B) The shuttle would turn around and fly backwards.
    (C) The shuttle would be very badly damaged.
    (D) The shuttle would be painted.

Check-up

A. Choose the correct answers.

1. A conversation content question asks

   (A) what the speaker's emotion, attitude, or opinion is
   (B) why the speaker has said something
   (C) for explicit details or facts from the conversation to be identified
   (D) about the relationship of ideas in a conversation

2. A lecture content question asks

   (A) what the lecture is about or why it is being given
   (B) what the speaker's emotion, attitude, or opinion is
   (C) about the relationship of ideas in a lecture
   (D) why the speaker has said something

Key Vocabulary Practice

B. Fill in the blanks with the correct words.

classmates	outline	absent	Earth	cosmic	space

1. In group projects students have to work with their _____.

2. If students are _____ from too many classes, they will miss important lessons.

3. An _____ shows the plan and process needed to complete a project.

4. _____ rays are affecting the Earth's temperatures.

5. We live on planet _____.

6. Clouds bounce heat from the sun back into _____.

[Review 1]

Conversation 1

🎧 Listen to the conversation and take notes. **Track 1-57**

Man - Student	Woman - Professor
• He is in the professor's _____ _____	
• Has missed a lot of classes because _____ _____ _____ _____ _____ _____	• Asks for doctors note • Is glad he _____ • Gives students _____ _____ _____ _____ _____

Choose the correct answers. **Track 1-58**

1. What are the speakers mainly discussing?

(A) The man's illness

(B) How the professor decides grades

(C) How to get caught up in class

(D) The importance of attending class

2. What is the woman's opinion of the student?

(A) She thinks he is lying

(B) She thinks he is very clever

(C) She thinks he needs help because the class is difficult

(D) She thinks he is good for trying to catch up

3. Why does the professor ask for a list of classes the student has missed?

(A) So she can give him handouts from those classes

(B) So she can write it down

(C) To check his doctor's note

(D) To check if he has missed anything important

4. Which of the following is NOT advice that the professor gave to the student?

(A) Look over the lecture summaries

(B) Get lecture notes from a classmate

(C) See a doctor about your cold

(D) See me if you have any problems

Listen to the lecture and take notes. **Track 1-59**

Impressionism

- Color
- Movement
- Light

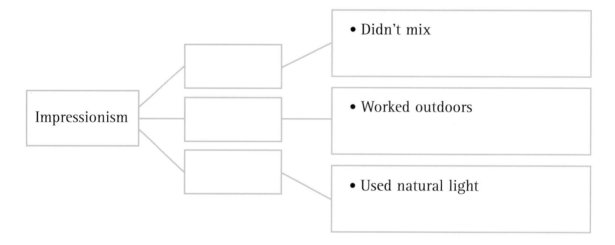

Impressionism

- Didn't mix
- Worked outdoors
- Used natural light

Choose the correct answers. **Track 1-60**

1. What is the lecture mainly about?

(A) The Impressionist painters and their work
(B) Why people didn't like Impressionism
(C) How people posed in Impressionist paintings
(D) The key features of Impressionist painting

2. How did Impressionist art differ from previous art?

(A) It featured people instead of landscapes.
(B) It used new and different blends of colors.
(C) It created a three-dimensional effect.
(D) It was created outside using natural light.

3. What is the speaker's opinion of Impressionism?

    (A) He likes it because it is different.

    (B) He likes it because the colors blend so well.

    (C) He thinks it's difficult because it uses natural light.

    (D) He doesn't like it because it's blurry.

4. How are the points in the lecture organized?

    (A) In the order that the painters painted

    (B) From most difficult to least difficult

    (C) In the order the textbook mentions them

    (D) By describing the most important points

5. Why does the professor say this: 🎧 ?

    (A) To show why older styles of art were better

    (B) To show how older styles of art were different

    (C) To explain how the students should paint

    (D) To describe a famous canvas

6. Which of the following is true of Impressionism? Place a checkmark in the correct box.

Statement	True	False
Rejected standards of the day		
Tried to exactly reproduce what they saw		
Always used indoor subjects		
Used natural light		
Blended colors		

🎧 **Listen to the lecture and take notes.** `Track 1-61`

Pandas

- Eat plants
- Live in small groups
- Do not hibernate
- Going extinct

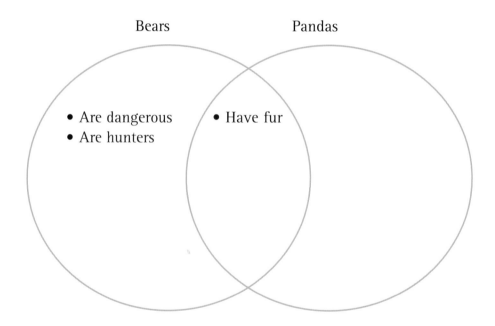

Bears   Pandas

- Are dangerous
- Are hunters

- Have fur

Choose the correct answers. `Track 1-62`

1. What is the talk mainly about?

(A) Why bears hibernate

(B) The causes of pandas going extinct

(C) The similarities and differences of panda bears and other bears

(D) The importance of saving pandas

2. How does the professor introduce the topic of panda bears?

   (A) By listing what they look like
   (B) By comparing them to other bears
   (C) By asking students to describe their behavior
   (D) By showing a picture of a panda bear in the wild

3. Which of the following was NOT mentioned as a cause of the panda decline?

   (A) Loss of homes
   (B) Hibernation
   (C) Having few babies
   (D) Hunting

4. What is the professor's attitude towards panda hunters?

   (A) She thinks they do a good job.
   (B) She thinks they are cruel.
   (C) She thinks they should hunt regular bears.
   (D) She thinks they are not as bad as companies that cut down trees.

Listen to part of the conversation again. Then answer the question.

5. Why does the professor say this: ?

   (A) To test students knowledge on bear behavior
   (B) To show students that it is always true
   (C) To show students that it is NOT always true
   (D) To test students on if they were listening

6. Choose whether each of the following is true of pandas, other bears, or both.

Statement	Pandas	Other Bears	Both
Protective of young			
Hunt for food			
Eat mainly plants			
Hibernate in winter months			
Have few babies			

Lecture 3

Listen to the lecture and take notes. **Track 1-63**

Physics 101

- Electricity

- Nuclear Power

- Microwaves

Physics 101

Problem	Solution
• Everything stopped when the sun went down →	
• Using oil to heat homes was not clean →	
• Took long time to heat food →	
• Difficult to send TV pictures →	

Choose the correct answers. **Track 1-64**

1. What is the talk mainly about?

(A) Their first major assignment for their physics class
(B) How technology can often cause more problems
(C) Different types of physics
(D) How physics has solved various problems

2. Why does the professor mention electricity?

    (A) To introduce the topic of today's lecture

    (B) To remind students that they should understand it for the test

    (C) Because it was studied last week

    (D) As an example of one way that physics has changed our lives

3. Which of the following is mentioned as something that pollutes the air?

    (A) Electricity   (B) Oil heating

    (C) Nuclear power   (D) Microwaves

Listen again to part of the lecture. Then answer the question. ◯

4. What is the professor's attitude towards nuclear power?

    (A) She thinks it was not a good solution.

    (B) She thinks it is very safe.

    (C) She thinks it is good because we also got nuclear weapons.

    (D) She thinks it is very interesting.

5. Why does the professor say this: ◯ ?

    (A) To encourage students to think of other types of ovens

    (B) To suggest another use for the microwave oven

    (C) To get students to think about ideas for project topics

    (D) To remind them that microwaves are not only used in microwave ovens

6. Indicate whether each of the following was mentioned in the talk.

Statement	YES	NO
The class is Physics 101.		
Electricity made it practical to do business after dark.		
Nuclear power gives clean energy.		
Nuclear power gives safe energy.		
Microwaves ovens are good for news reporters.		

Listen to the lecture and take notes. Track 1-65

Woman - Student	Man - University Employee
• Wants to borrow _____ • Her professor said _____ _____ _____ _____ _____ _____ _____	• It is a _____ _____ • Tells student she can do __ _____ _____ _____ _____ _____

Choose the correct answers. Track 1-66

1. What are the speakers mainly discussing?

(A) What kind of books to use for doing research
(B) How to use the university library
(C) Why due dates are different for different types of books
(D) How to use the new computerized database

2. According to the conversation, which of the following can the student borrow?

(A) Reference material
(B) Journal articles
(C) Novels
(D) Nothing

3. Why does the man say this: ◯ ?

(A) To imply that the library is under funded
(B) To suggest that he agrees with the student
(C) To convince the student to return her late book
(D) To explain why she can't borrow all the books

4. What information is true about reference material and novels?
For each phrase below, place a checkmark in correct column.

	Reference Material	Novels
Cannot be removed from library		
Will be scanned by librarian		
Can be borrowed for up to three weeks		
Can be viewed upon showing Student ID		

[07] Conversation

Getting Ready to Listen

A. Learn the words.

Key Vocabulary

locker	a small metal box for personal possessions that can be shut and locked
membership	an official way to belong to a club or group
court	the playing field for a game of tennis

TOEFL® Vocabulary

public	open for the use of the community
fee	the price to enter an organization or facility
tend	to be likely to do something
lend	to give something that you expect to be returned
reserve	to ask that a position or product be held

B. Learn the question type.

TOEFL® Question Type

Main Idea

What problem does the man/woman have?

What is the conversation mainly about?

Why is the man/woman talking to the professor/librarian/etc?

- This type of question is asking about what the conversation is mainly about or why the speakers are having the conversation (having a problem, asking a question, etc.)
- The answer should NOT include portions of the conversation.

Practice

Track 2-1

A. Listen to the first part of the conversation and choose the correct answers.

1. What is the main topic of this conversation?

   (A) Places to go for new students

   (B) How to get started at the sports center

2. How does the man explain what the student needs to do?

   (A) He lists what to do.

   (B) He compares different types of sports.

Note-taking

B. Listen to the full conversation and take notes. Track 2-2

Woman - Student	Man - Sports Center Employee
• Wants to use the _____ _____ _____ _____ _____ _____ _____ • Decides to _____ _____	• Needs to do two things: open an account and _____ _____ • Show student ID and he _____ _____ • Is open to _____ • People tend to _____ _____ • Can pay to _____ • Will lend _____ _____ • If she wants to _____ _____

C. Choose the correct answers.

1. Why does the student go to the sports center?

    (A) She wants to learn about joining the center.

    (B) She wants to ask about taking exercise classes.

2. What are the speakers mainly discussing?

    (A) Which parts of the center the students use most often

    (B) What the student has to do to get a membership

3. What does the man imply about the lockers?

    (A) That the student should get one each visit

    (B) That the student should get one that is only hers

TOEFL® Vocabulary Practice

D. Fill in the blanks with the correct words.

lend	reserved	public	fees	tend

1. _____ buildings and parks are open to everyone.

2. People _____ to do the same routines when they go to the gym.

3. Gyms will often _____ members a towel when they work out.

4. Each year people must pay yearly membership _____ to the clubs that they belong to.

5. A plane ticket must be _____ in order to ensure the person has a seat on a plane.

Test

Listen to the conversation and take notes. **Track 2-3**

Man - Student	Woman - Sport Center Employee
• Would like to reserve _____ _____ • Has a gym _____ _____ _____ _____ _____ _____ _____ _____ _____	• Two ways _____ • Can reserve in _____ _____ • They are open to _____ _____ _____ _____ _____ _____ _____

Choose the correct answers. **Track 2-4**

1. What problem does the man need help with?

(A) He needs information about playing tennis there.
(B) He wants to get a gym membership.
(C) He is interested in taking tennis lessons.
(D) He is looking for a partner to play tennis with.

2. When are the tennis courts the busiest?

(A) During tournaments   (B) On weekends
(C) In the mornings and evenings   (D) Every day after five

3. What can be inferred about why the gym gets busy?

(A) Because the fees are low
(B) Because they built a new swimming pool
(C) Because of the traffic at that time of day
(D) Because people are going before or after work

4. What can you infer from the man's response?

(A) He likes tennis and plans to use the courts often.
(B) He is too busy to play much tennis.
(C) He has been sick lately, so he has not played much.
(D) He thinks that he has a chance to play for his school's team.

Lecture - Literature

Getting Ready to Listen

A. Learn the words.

Key Vocabulary

grow up	to be on the process of becoming an adult
teenager	someone who is between the ages of 13 and 19
adult	someone who is fully grown up

TOEFL® Vocabulary

theme	main idea
criticize	to find problems or faults in someone or something
experience	to live through a situation
remain	to stay behind; to stay the same
escape	to get away from

B. Learn the question type.

TOEFL® Question Type

Main Idea

What is the main idea of the lecture?

What is the lecture mainly about?

- This type of question is asking about what the lecture is mainly about or why it is being given (introduce a new topic, expand on a previously discussed issue, etc.)
- The answer should NOT include portions of the lecture.

Practice

A. **Listen to the first part of the lecture and choose the correct answers.** `Track 2-5`

1. What is the main topic in this lecture?

   (A) *The Catcher in the Rye*   (B) *To Kill a Mockingbird*

2. What are the key points in this lecture?

   (A) The main character criticizes people, wants to protect younger people, and has difficulty becoming an adult.

   (B) The main character is a teenager, is a boy, and likes *To Kill a Mockingbird*

3. How does the professor describe the main topic?

   (A) By giving examples of similar books

   (B) By explaining the themes in the book

4. Choose the best note-taking diagram for this lecture.

   (A) Concept Defining Diagram   (B) Cause and Effect Diagram   (C) Venn Diagram

Note-taking

B. **Draw the diagram chosen in question 4. Then insert the information from questions 1 and 2.**

C. **Now listen to the full lecture and complete your notes.** `Track 2-6`

D. Choose the correct answers.

1. What is the lecture mainly about?

(A) The main character's problems

(B) The author's problems

2. What is the main point of this lecture?

(A) The lessons that can be learned from *The Catcher and the Rye*

(B) The impact of *The Catcher and the Rye's* story upon people

3. What is the likely outcome of reading *The Catcher in the Rye*?

(A) Understanding the main character and feeling sorry for him

(B) Feeling confused about the book and disliking the main character

TOEFL® Vocabulary Practice

E. Fill in the blanks with the correct words.

theme	criticize	escape	remaining	experiences

1. Movie reviews often _____ movies that people do not like.

2. The difficult _____ of a teenager are all part of growing up.

3. Prisoners often think about how to _____ from jail.

4. Every movie has a _____ which the whole story focuses on.

5. There is often a lot of food _____ after a buffet dinner.

Listen to the lecture and take notes. **Track 2-7**

The Watership Down's Themes

- **People**
  - can't get along or accept differences

- **Politics**
  - no government is perfect

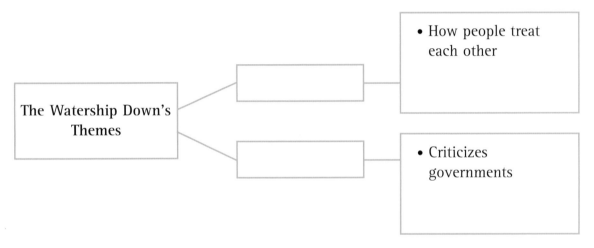

The Watership Down's Themes

- How people treat each other

- Criticizes governments

Choose the correct answers. **Track 2-8**

1. What is the lecture mainly about?

(A) The writer of *Watership Down*

(B) The main characters of *Watership Down*

(C) The themes of *Watership Down*

(D) The political ideas behind *Watership Down*

2. What is the reason the rabbits leave home?

(A) They do not have any freedom.

(B) Their home is going to be destroyed.

(C) They want to have an adventure.

(D) They want a new government.

Listen again to part of the lecture. Then answer the question.

3. Why does the professor mention the leader of Efrafa?

    (A) To show the government style of Efrafa

    (B) To compare Efrafa and the Tharn Warren

    (C) To describe how the rabbits typically acted

    (D) To show that the rabbits lived peacefully with others

4. How is the professor's lecture organized?

    (A) The themes of the story and how they are shown

    (B) The characters and then what the themes are

    (C) The character comparisons followed by the contrasts

    (D) The steps the author took in writing the book

Listen again to part of the lecture. Then answer the question.

5. What is the professor's attitude towards *Watership Down*?

    (A) He thinks that it shows real life very well.

    (B) He believes that *Watership Down* is a very simple book.

    (C) He thinks that the book is just about rabbits.

    (D) He thinks that it is hard to understand.

6. Which of the following is true of *Watership Down*? Place a checkmark in the correct box.

Statements	True	False
The rabbits want to find a brand new place to live.		
They leave their home because it will be destroyed.		
There are two other groups that the rabbits fight with.		
Some people suggest that the rabbit towns are like businesses.		

Check-up

A. Choose the correct answers.

1. A main idea question asks

   (A) what the conversation is about or why the speakers are having the conversation
   (B) about the relationship of ideas in a conversation
   (C) why the speaker has said something
   (D) what the speaker's emotion, attitude, or opinion is

2. A main idea question asks

   (A) what the speaker's emotion, attitude, or opinion is
   (B) what the lecture is about or why it is being given
   (C) for explicit details or facts from the lecture to be identified
   (D) about the relationship of ideas in a lecture

Key Vocabulary Practice

B. Fill in the blanks with the correct words.

courts	locker	membership	grow up
	adults	teenager	

1. A _____ is a good place to store personal belongings while swimming.

2. Most people consider 20-year-olds to be _____.

3. Tennis is played on many different _____ such as grass, clay, and concrete.

4. A gym will usually only allow people with a _____ to enter.

5. Some people believe that being a _____ is the most difficult time in life.

6. Each experience a child has helps them _____.

[08] Conversation

Getting Ready to Listen

A. Learn the words.

Key Vocabulary

service	work done for others
chess	a strategic board game played by two players with 16 pieces each
elderly	old people

TOEFL® Vocabulary

additionally	besides; in addition to
community	a social group of any size whose members reside in a specific locality
president	the leader of a group; head of the government in a Republic
elect	to choose someone by voting
local	of or relating to a particular area; nearby

B. Learn the question type.

TOEFL® Question Type

Detail

According to the man/woman, what is X?

What are X?

- This type of question is asking for explicit details or facts from the conversation to be identified.
- The answer will usually be consistent with the main idea of the conversation.

Practice

 A. Listen to the first part of the conversation and choose the correct answers.

Track 2-9

1. What is the main topic in this conversation?

   (A) How to meet new people at school
   (B) What club choices the school offers

2. How does the man answer the student?

   (A) He describes the different types of clubs
   (B) He tells which club is better to join

Note-taking

B. Listen to the full conversation and take notes. Track 2-10

Woman - Student	Man - Activities Director
• Just moved and would like to _____ _____ • Was president of _____ _____ • Would like to do _____ _____ • Would like to _____ _____ _____	• Have two types of clubs: _____ _____ _____ • Need to choose a club then _____ _____ • Chess club is going to _____ _____ • Community service clubs _____ _____ _____ • Thinks it's _____ _____

C. Choose the correct answers.

1. What was the conversation mainly about?

(A) Deciding on a club to join   (B) Joining a chess club

2. According to the man, what do people who join community service clubs do?

(A) They play sports with kids.

(B) They help other people.

3. What position was the student elected to in her old school?

(A) Vice president of her class

(B) President of the chess club

TOEFL® Vocabulary Practice

D. Fill in the blanks with the correct words.

additional	president	elected	community	local

1. The _____ of the club is the person who is in charge.

2. In the United States, a president is _____ every four years.

3. The closest place to rent a movie is usually the _____ video shop.

4. The _____ center is a good place to find out what activities are happening in that area.

5. People who work overtime usually receive _____ money on their pay check.

Test

Listen to the conversation and take notes. **Track 2-11**

Man - Student	Woman - Professor
• Asks if she helps the _____ _____	
• Asks who they elected as _____	• Was close but Justin was __ _____ _____
• Is interested in joining ____ _____ _____ _____ _____ _____ _____ _____ _____	_____ _____ _____ _____ _____ _____

Choose the correct answers. **Track 2-12**

1. What problem does the student need help with?

(A) He wants to meet new people at school.

(B) He wants to know where he can find a list of clubs.

(C) He needs information about a school sports team.

(D) He is looking for a study group to join.

2. Why does the woman say this: 🎧 ?

(A) She is explaining that the voting took place close by.

(B) She wants him to run for president.

(C) She doesn't like Justin.

(D) She wants to show someone else was nearly elected.

3. Where is the sports office located on campus?

(A) Near the computer lab   (B) Across from the soccer field

(C) Next to the health center   (D) Next to the dorms

4. Why does the woman mention the elderly?

(A) To give an example of who the community service club works with

(B) To explain that she spends time with her parents

(C) To complain about how boring the club activities are

(D) To describe who are members of social service clubs

Lecture - Environment

Getting Ready to Listen

A. Learn the words.

Key Vocabulary

landfill	a place where garbage is buried between layers of dirt
waste	material that is thrown away
space	the area that something can occupy

TOEFL® Vocabulary

recycle	to use again
compare	to look at the characteristics of two different things
method	a specific way of doing something
similarity	a characteristic that is the same for two different things
environment	the area in which something lives and that affects the health, growth, and development of such living things

B. Learn the question type.

TOEFL® Question Type

Detail

According to the professor, what is X?

What are X?

- This type of question is asking for explicit details or facts from the lecture to be identified.
- The answer will usually be consistent with the main idea of the lecture.

Practice

A. **Listen to the first part of the lecture and choose the correct answers.** `Track 2-13`

1. What is the main topic in this lecture?

   (A) Similarities and differences between two types of waste removal

   (B) Different methods that we can use to save the environment

2. What are the key points in this lecture?

   (A) Both recycling and landfills can pollute the environment.

   (B) There are two methods for dealing with garbage; landfills and recycling

3. How does the professor describe the main topic?

   (A) By comparing and contrasting landfills and recycling

   (B) By putting the steps of waste removal in order

4. Choose the best note-taking diagram for this lecture.

   (A) Problem and Solution   (B) Venn Diagram   (C) Ordering Diagram
                                                                   Diagram

Note-taking

B. **Draw the diagram chosen in question 4. Then insert the information from questions 1 and 2.**

C. **Now listen to the full lecture and complete your notes.** `Track 2-14`

D. Choose the correct answers.

1. What is the conversation mainly about?

(A) The differences between landfills and recycling

(B) The difference between garbage and waste

2. According to the professor, which of the following is true?

(A) There is no room left for landfills.

(B) Landfills take up a lot of space.

3. According to the professor, which of the following can be both dumped and recycled?

(A) Cans and newspapers   (B) Food and drinks

TOEFL® Vocabulary Practice

E. Fill in the blanks with the correct words.

recycled	compares	methods	similarities	environment

1. Pollution and garbage are causing problems in our _____.

2. Most cultures have different _____ of cooking.

3. There are certain things that can be _____ such as paper and plastic bottles.

4. Some of the basic _____ among all people is the need for food, water, and shelter.

5. A customer often _____ prices before buying a product.

Test

Listen to the lecture and take notes. `Track 2-15`

Energy Sources

- Wind
- Will last forever

- Coal
- Will run out

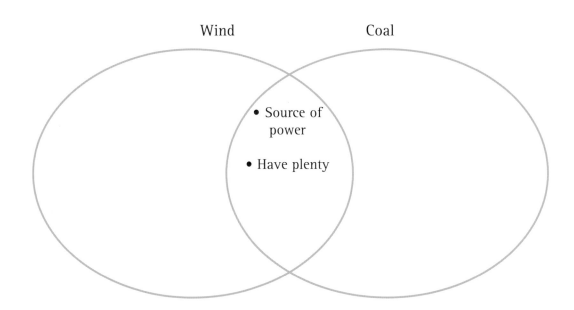

Wind   Coal

- Source of power
- Have plenty

Choose the correct answers. `Track 2-16`

1. What is the lecture about?

(A) The benefits of using coal for energy
(B) Large windmills that are used for power
(C) A comparison of energy sources
(D) The dangers of pollution

2. Why does the professor mention gases that are released from burning coal?

    (A) To explain how they are used for power

    (B) To show how coal pollutes the environment

    (C) To compare them to the gases from wind power

    (D) To describe how coal is the better fuel source

3. What does the professor say about wind power as an energy source?

    (A) It is being used in every country.

    (B) It is expensive.

    (C) It is less effective than coal.

    (D) It will never run out.

Listen again to part of the lecture. Then answer the question. ( )

4. Why does the professor say this: ( ) ?

    (A) To suggest that there is an enormous supply of coal

    (B) To emphasize that that wind power will last much longer

    (C) To explain how coal burns for a long time

    (D) To show how much he likes wind power

Listen again to part of the lecture. Then answer the question. ( )

5. What is the professor's opinion of wind power?

    (A) She does not think that it will cost more.

    (B) She wants to continue using coal until wind power is more developed.

    (C) She feels that it is not as effective as using coal.

    (D) She thinks that it is a better energy source than coal.

6. What can be inferred about coal and pollution?

    (A) Burning coal has caused a lot of pollution over the years.

    (B) The pollution has been limited by laws.

    (C) The pollution from coal has no effect on the Earth.

    (D) In the future we will be able to reduce its pollution.

Check-up

A. Choose the correct answers.

1. A conversation detail question asks

   (A) why the speaker has said something
   (B) for explicit details or facts from the conversation to be identified
   (C) what the speaker's emotion, attitude, or opinion is
   (D) about the relationship of ideas in a conversation

2. A lecture detail question asks

   (A) for explicit details or facts from the lecture to be identified
   (B) about the relationship of ideas in a lecture
   (C) what the lecture is about or why it is being given
   (D) why the speaker has said something

Key Vocabulary Practice

B. Fill in the blanks with the correct words.

service	elderly	chess	landfills	waste	space

1. _____ is a game enjoyed by many people.

2. Most people throw their _____ into garbage cans.

3. Garbage is often stored in _____.

4. The _____ often have to move into special homes.

5. Many charity groups provide a _____ to their local community.

6. People who collect many things often have very little _____ in their houses.

[09] Conversation

Getting Ready to Listen

A. Learn the words.

Key Vocabulary

calm	quiet; not nervous
copy	to make something that is the exact same as the original
fresh	recent; new

TOEFL® Vocabulary

confuse	to make unclear
delay	to wait; postpone
review	to look over something again
repetition	repeat; do over
interrupt	to cause a break in

B. Learn the question type.

TOEFL® Question Type

Function

What does the man/woman imply when he/she says this: ( ) ?

What does the man/woman mean when he/she says this: ( ) ?

Why does the man/woman say this: ( ) ?

You will hear part of the conversation again.

- This type of question is asking why the speaker has said something; it may not match what he/she directly states.
- To get the correct answer, tone of voice, stress on a certain word or phrase, or intonation should be paid close attention to.

Practice

A. Listen to the first part of the conversation and choose the correct answers.

Track 2-17

1. What is the main topic in this conversation?

   (A) A student's reasons for missing classes
   (B) Ways to remember class lessons better

2. How does the student explain the problem?

   (A) By describing what he can't do
   (B) By comparing two instructor's methods

Note-taking

B. Listen to the full conversation and take notes. Track 2-18

Man - Student	Man - Professor
• Needs _____ • Is having _____ • Does best to _____ • When the lecture _____ _____ _____ _____ _____	• Tells the student _____ _____ • Work on _____ _____ • Stay calm and _____ • Take notes on _____ _____ • Write them in own _____ • When the lecture is finished, _____ _____ • Repetition _____ • Can ask questions but _____ _____

C. Choose the correct answers.

Listen again to part of the conversation. Then answer the question. 🎧 **Track 2-19**

1. Why does the professor say this: 🎧 ?

   (A) She is going to give the student a good grade.
   (B) She knows how to help the student.

Listen again to part of the conversation. Then answer the question. 🎧 **Track 2-20**

2. Why does the professor say this: 🎧 ?

   (A) To explain what she means by the word 'repetition'
   (B) To suggest that the student will not pass if he doesn't work harder

3. What should the student do when taking notes?

   (A) Take notes on the main ideas
   (B) Copy what the professor says

TOEFL® Vocabulary Practice

D. Fill in the blanks with the correct words.

confuse	delayed	interrupt	repetition	review

1. Professors who talk too fast during lectures often _____ their students.

2. Before a test students usually _____ all the notes they took during lectures.

3. Professors often dislike when students _____ their lectures.

4. Learning by _____ means saying, doing, hearing, or seeing things many times.

5. A _____ flight will arrive later than expected.

Test

🎧 Listen to the conversation and take notes. `Track 2-21`

Woman - Student	Man - Professor
• Is struggling in _____ • Is taking a lot of _____ _____ _____ • Doesn't understand _____ _____ _____ _____ _____ _____ _____	• Asks if he is too _____ _____ • Thinks chemistry _____ • Write notes in _____ _____ _____ _____ _____ _____

Choose the correct answers. `Track 2-22`

1. Why does the student need help?

   (A) She is looking for additional work to keep her busy.

   (B) She is having a hard time with the lectures.

   (C) She wants to start tutoring students who are struggling.

   (D) She is trying to change classes.

2. According to the professor, what is the likely outcome of joining a study group?

   (A) Her grade will get worse.

   (B) Other students will give her a new way of looking at the problems.

   (C) The other students will tell her the answers.

   (D) The other students know more than the professor.

3. Why does the professor say this: 🎧 ?

   (A) To suggest that the student should focus on her best subject

   (B) To explain how she is often confused by chemistry

   (C) To imply that the student should think about taking an easier class

   (D) To suggest that it is not unusual to struggle with the subject

4. When does the study group meet?

   (A) Right after class   (B) On weekend mornings

   (C) During lunch   (D) During the evenings

Lecture - Health

Getting Ready to Listen

A. Learn the words.

Key Vocabulary

rinse	to wash lightly
scrub	to clean with hard rubbing
bacteria	tiny living organisms that can sometimes make you sick

TOEFL® Vocabulary

remind	to help someone to remember something
thorough	very complete
remove	get rid of
substance	something that has mass and occupies space
layer	a covering of some material laid or spread over a surface

B. Learn the question type.

TOEFL® Question Type

Function

What does the professor imply when he/she says this: ( ) ?

What does the professor mean when he/she says this: ( ) ?

Why does the professor say this: ( ) ?

You will hear part of the lecture again.

- This type of question is asking why the speaker has said something; it may not match what he/she directly states.
- To get the correct answer, tone of voice, stress on a certain word or phrase or intonation should be paid close attention to.

Practice

A. **Listen to the first part of the lecture and choose the correct answers.** `Track 2-23`

1. What is the main topic of this lecture?

   (A) Killing germs   (B) Getting sick

2. What are the key points in this lecture?

   (A) Germs get on hands and in mouths, to kill them hands should be washed with soap and water.

   (B) Some germs are harder to kill than others, so hands should never be washed.

3. How does the professor describe the main topic?

   (A) By comparing and contrasting   (B) By giving a problem and solution

4. Choose the best note-taking diagram for this lecture.

   (A) Venn Diagram   (B) Ordering Diagram   (C) Problem and Solution Diagram

---

Note-taking

B. **Draw the diagram chosen in question 4. Then insert the information from questions 1 and 2.**

C. **Now listen to the full lecture and complete your notes.** `Track 2-24`

D. Choose the correct answers.

1. What does the professor imply when he says this: ◯ ? **Track 2-25**

    (A) You have to do more than use soap and water to get your hands clean.
    (B) Washing your hands for a long time does not always kill germs.

2. Why does the professor say this: ◯ ? **Track 2-26**

    (A) To explain how hard it is to wash your hands and sing at the same time
    (B) To emphasize how well scrubbing your hands kills germs

3. According to the professor, how long should you scrub your hands for?

    (A) For as long as it takes to sing "Happy Birthday"
    (B) For as long as it takes to say "Happy Birthday"

TOEFL® Vocabulary Practice

E. Fill in the blanks with the correct words.

reminded	thorough	remove	substance	layers

1. Children often need to be _____ to brush their teeth.

2. A cake can have many different _____.

3. White glue is a _____ that comes off easily with soap and water.

4. A _____ review of one's notes is often the best way to get a good grade on an exam.

5. It is important to scrub one's hands hard in order to _____ the bacteria.

Test

🎧 Listen to the lecture and take notes. **Track 2-27**

Antibacterial Gels

- Don't use too often

- Rinse off

- Use normal soap more often

Antibacterial Gels

Problem	Solution
• Bad for hands → • Makes germs stronger →	

Choose the correct answers. **Track 2-28**

1. What is the lecture about?

(A) Cleaning products that kill germs

(B) How antibacterial gels aren't always helpful

(C) The importance of washing hair and skin

(D) How antibacterial gels are better than soaps

2. Why does the professor mention regular soap?

    (A) To convince the students to wash before they eat
    (B) To emphasize how gels kill more germs than soap
    (C) To show another way that people can kill germs
    (D) To describe how soap and gels are very similar

Listen again to part of the lecture. Then answer the question.

3. Why does the professor say this: ?

    (A) To emphasize how the gels are helpful
    (B) To explain that gels can be bad for your hands
    (C) To explain how he uses antibacterial gels
    (D) To compare the antibacterial gels to antibacterial soaps

4. What does the professor say about the chemicals that are used in antibacterial gels?

    (A) They can easily be washed off of your hands.
    (B) They build a protective layer on your hands.
    (C) They are like the chemicals used in regular soap.
    (D) They can actually do bad things to your hands.

5. What is the professor's opinion of antibacterial gels?

    (A) He thinks that they are fine for healthy people to use.
    (B) He believes that they are just as good as regular soap.
    (C) He feels they cause problems and are not necessary.
    (D) He thinks that no one will be using them in the future.

6. What can be inferred about antibacterial gels?

    (A) They are fine in small amounts.
    (B) They are just as good as regular soaps.
    (C) They don't last as long as soaps.
    (D) They are more expensive than soaps.

Check-up

A. Choose the correct answers.

1. A conversation function question asks

    (A) what the speaker's emotion, attitude, or opinion is

    (B) about the relationship of ideas in a conversation

    (C) for explicit details or facts from the conversation to be identified

    (D) why the speaker has said something

2. A lecture function question asks

    (A) why the speaker has said something

    (B) for explicit details or facts from the lecture to be identified

    (C) what the lecture is about or why it is being given

    (D) what the speaker's emotion, attitude, or opinion is

Key Vocabulary Practice

B. Fill in the blanks with the correct words.

rinsing	scrub	bacteria	fresh	copy	calm

1. Doctors _____ their hands and arms for a long time before surgery.

2. _____ with a strong mouthwash can kill germs inside the mouth.

3. Not all _____ cause sickness; some are important for good health.

4. It is helpful to review lecture notes, while the information is still _____.

5. To repeat, write, or draw something exactly is to _____ it.

6. Students often find it difficult to stay _____ when taking exams.

[10] Conversation

Getting Ready to Listen

A. Learn the words.

Key Vocabulary

post	to display in public view
menu	a list of food available at a place that serves food
taste	a personal preference

TOEFL® Vocabulary

cafeteria	a room where people can buy food and eat meals
schedule	a list of times when things are being done
wonder	to be curious about something
complain	to express feelings of unhappiness
credit	a system of points to represent money, often to replace cash exchanges and simplify payment processes

B. Learn the question type.

TOEFL® Question Type

Attitude

What is the man/woman's attitude towards X?

What is the man/woman's opinion of X?

• This type of question is asking what the speaker's emotion, attitude, or opinion is; it may not match what he/she directly states.

• To get the correct answer, tone of voice, stress on a certain word or phrase, or intonation should be paid close attention to.

• Some questions will replay part of the conversation again.

Practice

A. **Listen to the first part of the conversation and choose the correct answers.**

Track 2-29

1. What is the main topic of this conversation?

    (A) How the cafeteria works

    (B) What types of food the cafeteria serves

2. How did the woman explain how the cafeteria woks?

    (A) By giving specific information

    (B) By comparing and contrasting

Note-taking

B. **Listen to the full conversation and take notes.** Track 2-30

Man - Student	Woman - Cafeteria Employee
• Is new and is not _____ _____	• Tell the student he needs to know two things: _____ _____ • It is open for _____ _____ • Hours are posted on _____ _____ • Menu is on _____ • Laughs and says everyone's _____ _____ • Should bring _____ • Can pay cash or _____ • Each meals takes _____ _____ • This is _____
• Asks if many students _____ _____	

C. Choose the correct answers.

Listen again to part of the conversation. Then answer the question. ◯ **Track 2-31**

1. What is the woman's opinion about the food?

(A) She thinks the food is good but that some people still complain.

(B) She thinks the food is very bad and everyone complains.

2. What is the student's opinion of the cafeteria?

(A) He thinks they should have more types of food.

(B) He thinks it is a good system.

3. Why does the woman say this: ◯ ? **Track 2-32**

(A) To get him to take the meal plan

(B) To explain that the meal plan is terrible

TOEFL® Vocabulary Practice

D. Fill in the blanks with the correct words.

cafeteria	schedule	wonder	complain	credit

1. A _____ tells people when and where events are happening.

2. When people don't like the service in a hotel, they sometimes _____ to the manager.

3. A cafeteria will often use a _____ system instead of cash to save time when people are buying food.

4. Children often _____ about things that are new to them.

5. Many students eat their lunches in the school _____.

Test

🎧 Listen to the conversation and take notes. **Track 2-33**

Woman - Student	Man - Cafeteria
• Wants to know about ____ _____ _____ _____ _____ _____ _____ _____ _____ _____ _____	• Have two choices: _____ _____ • The grill is open _____ • Hamburgers, _____ _____ • The daily meal changes ___ _____ _____ _____ _____ _____ _____

Choose the correct answers. **Track 2-34**

1. Why is the student talking to the cafeteria employee?

(A) She is hungry and wants something to eat.

(B) She wants information about the cafeteria food.

(C) She is trying to find a place to study.

(D) She is looking for one of his teachers.

2. What type of food is NOT mentioned as being served by the grill?

(A) Hot dog　　　　　　　　(B) Hamburger

(C) Chicken　　　　　　　　(D) Fish

3. What is the student's opinion of vegetables?

(A) She likes to eat them, but not too often.

(B) She loves them.

(C) She does not enjoy eating them.

(D) She likes them more than fruit.

4. How does the woman explain how the grill works?

(A) By listing the rules for cooking on the grill

(B) By cooking food

(C) By describing the cooking methods

(D) By giving the student examples

Lecture - Technology

Getting Ready to Listen

A. Learn the words.

Key Vocabulary

three-dimensional	having height, width, and depth; often shortened to 3D
model	an example version of something to give the general impression of the actual product
signature	a person's name, as written by the person

TOEFL® Vocabulary

image	a visual representation of something
project	to cause an image to appear using light
regular	usual or normal
faculty	a group of teachers
prove	to show something is true

B. Learn the question type.

TOEFL® Question Type

Attitude

What is the professor's attitude towards X?

What is the professor's opinion of X?

- This type of question is asking what the speaker's emotion, attitude, or opinion is; it may not match what he/she directly states.
- To get the correct answer, tone of voice, stress on a certain word or phrase, or intonation should be paid close attention to.
- Some questions will replay part of the lecture again.

Practice

A. Listen to the first part of the lecture and choose the correct answers. `Track 2-35`

1. What is the main topic of this lecture?

   (A) How holograms are made   (B) Different uses for holograms

2. What are the key points in this lecture?

   (A) Holograms are used in advertising and crime fighting.
   (B) There are good things and bad things about using holograms.

3. How does the professor describe the main topic?

   (A) By categorizing uses of holograms
   (B) By describing the steps to make holograms

4. Choose the best note-taking diagram for this lecture.

   (A) Ordering Diagram   (B) Problem and Solution   (C) Categorizing Diagram
                                                            Diagram

Note-taking

B. Draw the diagram chosen in question 4. Then insert the information from questions 1 and 2.

C. Now listen to the full lecture and complete your notes. `Track 2-36`

D. Choose the correct answers.

Listen again to part of the lecture. Then answer the question. ( ) [Track 2-37]

1. Why does the professor say this: ( )?

(A) To show that these are interesting ways to use holograms

(B) To show that he loves holograms

2. What is the professor's attitude about holograms?

(A) He thinks that they have many interesting, helpful uses.

(B) He thinks that they are good for marketing, but not preventing crime.

Listen again to part of the lecture. Then answer the question. ( ) [Track 2-38]

3. What is the professor's opinion about these car images?

(A) He thinks that they need to look better.

(B) He thinks that they help sell cars.

TOEFL® Vocabulary Practice

E. Fill in the blanks with the correct words.

regular	images	faculty	prove	project

1. Doctors look at x-ray _____ to see inside bodies.

2. Holograms used in advertising are designed to look just like the _____ product.

3. The _____ at a school are responsible for teaching the students.

4. Large film projectors in movie theaters _____ films on large screens.

5. Scientists used a variety of methods to _____ their theories.

Test

🎧 **Listen to the lecture and take notes.** `Track 2-39`

Robots in Hospitals

- ZEUS System - for viewing

- Da Vinci System - helps do surgery

```
              Robots in Hospitals
         ┌───────────────┴───────────────┐
    Zeus Robot                      Da Vinci Robot
┌─────────────────┐            ┌─────────────────────┐
│                 │            │                     │
│                 │            │                     │
│                 │            │                     │
│                 │            │                     │
│                 │            │                     │
└─────────────────┘            └─────────────────────┘
```

Choose the correct answers. `Track 2-40`

1. What is the lecture about?

    (A) How robots are saving hospitals money
    (B) How robots are replacing doctors
    (C) How some robots are better than others
    (D) How robots are being used in surgery

Listen again to part of the lecture. Then answer the question. ◯

2. Why does the professor say this: ◯?

    (A) To show that these robots help doctors

    (B) To show that the doctors don't need the robots

    (C) To show that the robots don't need the doctors

    (D) To show that the robots are not helpful

3. How does the ZEUS robot help doctors?

    (A) It helps them see things during surgery.

    (B) It helps them reach into smaller places.

    (C) It gives them better control over other robots.

    (D) It helps them do surgery faster.

Listen again to part of the lecture. Then answer the question. ◯

4. What is the professors opinion of the da Vinci robot?

    (A) He thinks it is better than other robots

    (B) He thinks it is funny

    (C) He thinks it is very useful for doctors

    (D) He likes them so much he wants one for himself

5. What can be inferred about the future role of robots in surgery?

    (A) They are not going to be used for much longer.

    (B) They will continue to help doctors.

    (C) They will only be used in the easiest surgeries.

    (D) They will become too expensive.

6. Why does the professor mention a joystick?

    (A) To show how hard it is to control a robot

    (B) To describe how the doctor controls the robot

    (C) To explain how doctors operate on robots

    (D) To show how the robot is used in emergencies

Check-up

A. Choose the correct answers.

1. A conversation attitude question asks

    (A) why the speaker has said something

    (B) about the relationship of ideas in a conversation

    (C) for explicit details or facts from the conversation to be identified

    (D) what the speaker's emotion, attitude, or opinion is

2. A lecture attitude question asks

    (A) what the speaker's emotion, attitude, or opinion is

    (B) what the lecture is about or why it is being given

    (C) for explicit details or facts from the lecture to be identified

    (D) why the speaker has said something

Key Vocabulary Practice

B. Fill in the blanks with the correct words.

post	menu	taste	three-dimensional
	model	signature	

1. A good _____ usually offers a variety of foods.

2. Most businesses _____ signs on their doors that give their opening hours.

3. A _____ car is often very similar to the actual car but much smaller.

4. Teenagers often have a different _____ in clothes than their parents.

5. Holograms are fascinating _____ images.

6. Everybody's _____ is different.

[11] Conversation

Getting Ready to Listen

A. Learn the words.

Key Vocabulary

roommate	someone that shares a living space with another person
part-time	part of the time
job	a post of employment

TOEFL® Vocabulary

dorm	a building where students live
rule	a formal order or regulation that must be followed
recommend	to suggest something
communicate	to speak or write to express thoughts and feelings
compromise	to settle a difference by having each side agree to do something for the other side

B. Learn the question type.

TOEFL® Question Type

Organization

How did the man/woman organize the information about X?

How is the discussion organized?

Why does the man/woman discuss X?

- This type of question is asking about the overall organization of the conversation or the relationship between two parts of the conversation.
- The answer may take into account what examples have been given or look at comparisons that have been made.

Practice

A. **Listen to the first part of the conversation and choose the correct answers.**
Track 2-41

1. What is the main topic of this conversation?

    (A) How to change dorm rooms
    (B) How to fix a problem with a roommate

2. How does the woman explain the solution?

    (A) By suggesting options to fix the problem
    (B) By describing the steps that must be taken to get a new room

Note-taking

B. **Listen to the full conversation and take notes.** Track 2-42

Man - Student	Woman - University Employee
• Needs to talk to _____ _____ • His roommate _____ _____ • Wants to _____ • Neither have tried to _____ _____ • Has a part-time job doing _____ _____ _____ • Thinks he could not watch _____ _____ _____	 • Can't let him _____ _____ • Can recommend _____ _____ • Communicate: it is not _____ _____ • Should reach an agreement about ____ _____ • Thinks _____ _____

C. Choose the correct answers.

1. Why does the student mention TV?

(A) To give an example of something he could compromise about

(B) To explain how much he prefers watching TV to being with his roommate

2. How did the woman organize information about the problem?

(A) She compared it to a similar situation she was in.

(B) She suggested possible ways to fix the problem.

3. What is the woman's attitude towards the student?

(A) She is sorry she can't let him change rooms.

(B) She is angry at him for watching TV.

TOEFL® Vocabulary Practice

D. Fill in the blanks with the correct words.

dorm	rules	recommend	communicate	compromise

1. In order to make two people happy, a _____ is often needed.

2. A telephone is a good way to _____ with someone when he or she lives far away.

3. Many _____ rooms have two beds, two desks, and one sink.

4. A librarian can often _____ a good book to read.

5. A dorm usually has _____ for when the students have to be quiet.

Test

Listen to the conversation and take notes. **Track 2-43**

Woman - Student	Man - University Employee
• Roommate and her thinking about _____	• Painting is against _____
• Was hoping for _____	• Can't compromise _____
	• Could decorate in _____

Choose the correct answers. **Track 2-44**

1. Why is the student talking to the man?

(A) She is looking for a new roommate.
(B) She wants to find some painting supplies.
(C) She wants to know if she can paint her room.
(D) She is thinking about moving out of her room.

2. What color was the student thinking about painting her room?

(A) Blue   (B) Yellow
(C) Pink   (D) Green

3. Why does the man mention that painting is against the rules?

(A) To suggest that many other students have been in trouble over painting
(B) To let the student know that if she does it, she will get in trouble
(C) To show the student that he is an adult, and he's in charge
(D) To try and tell her that she can do it, but she has to keep it a secret

4. Why does the woman say this: ◯ ?

(A) To let the man know that she will not paint her room
(B) To emphasize that he cannot tell her what to do
(C) To suggest that she try painting as a fun activity
(D) To hint that she'll paint her room the next year

Lecture - Geography

Getting Ready to Listen

A. Learn the words.

Key Vocabulary	
model	a description of a system or theory
split	to divide into smaller parts
transportation	a way to travel from one place to another

TOEFL® Vocabulary	
expand	to grow
area	a general district
develop	to improve
economy	the money that is earned or spent in a place
invest	to put money into something in the hope that it will create a bigger return of money

B. Learn the question type.

TOEFL® Question Type

Organization

How did the professor organize the information about X?

How is the discussion organized?

Why does the professor discuss X?

- This type of question is asking about the overall organization of the lecture or the relationship between two parts of the lecture.
- The answer will take into account what examples have been given or look at comparisons that have been made.

Practice

A. Listen to the first part of the lecture and choose the correct answers. `Track 2-45`

1. What is the main topic in this lecture?

   (A) Steps for city development   (B) The importance of the modern city

2. What are the key points in this lecture?

   (A) The downtown area, then the factory area, and then the living area must develop to make a city grow.

   (B) The center of the town must grow for a city to develop.

3. How does the professor describe the main topic?

   (A) By comparing and contrasting two cities

   (B) By describing the order of city development

4. Choose the best note-taking diagram for this lecture.

   (A) Venn Diagram   (B) Problem and Solution Diagram   (C) Ordering Diagram

Note-taking

B. Draw the diagram chosen in question 4. Then insert the information from questions 1 and 2.

C. Now listen to the full lecture and complete your notes. `Track 2-46`

D. Choose the correct answers.

1. How does the professor organize the lecture?

    (A) He lists modern examples of each part of the city

    (B) He gives the order of a city's development

2. Why does the professor mention transportation?

    (A) To give an example of how important the downtown area is

    (B) To show how it affects the development of the city

3. What is the professor's opinion of city development?

    (A) He thinks it's interesting

    (B) He thinks it's boring

TOEFL® Vocabulary Practice

E. Fill in the blanks with the correct words.

expands	area	develop	economy	invest

1. A rich city usually has a strong _____.

2. As a city _____, it needs better transportation.

3. Professional athletes take a lot of time to _____ their skills.

4. The _____ in the center of a city is usually where the most transportation is.

5. In order for a company to grow, people need to _____ their money in the company.

Test

Listen to the lecture and take notes. `Track 2-47`

Moldova

- Stable Economy
- Good School System
- Government Problems

Developing Country - Moldova

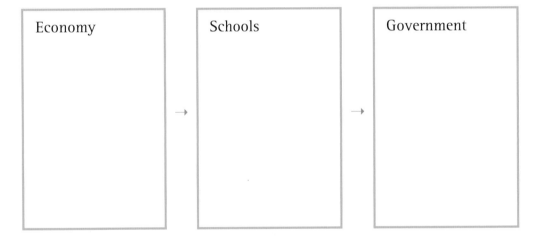

Economy	Schools	Government
→	→	

Choose the correct answers. `Track 2-48`

1. What is the lecture about?

(A) How Moldova is developing as a country
(B) The developing countries of Eastern Europe
(C) The importance of government in development
(D) Moldova's relationship with other countries

2. According to the professor, how did Moldova increase its economy?

(A) It brought in foreign investors.
(B) It sold farmland to the people.
(C) It made a strong government.
(D) It traded with other countries.

3. Why does the professor say this: ◯ ?

(A) To emphasize how these jobs are specifically chosen
(B) To explain that not all jobs are good enough for the students
(C) To describe how there are not many jobs in Moldova
(D) To suggest that the students like some jobs more than others

4. What is the professor's opinion of Moldova's economy and school system?

(A) He thinks the schools still need work.
(B) He feels they are both doing very well.
(C) He feels they are hurting Moldova's growth.
(D) He thinks the government needs to change them.

5. Why does the professor mention foreign investors?

(A) To explain how Moldova does not need them
(B) To support the idea that Moldova can compete with them
(C) To explain how economy is more important than education
(D) To give an example of one of Moldova's weaknesses

6. What can be inferred about the role that government plays in Moldova's development?

(A) It is the biggest reason for Moldova's fast development.
(B) It does not affect it as much as the economy does.
(C) It needs to pay more attention to the school systems.
(D) It is not helping Moldova's future in certain ways.

Check-up

Question Type Review

A. Choose the correct answers.

1. A conversation organization question asks
   - (A) what the speaker's emotion, attitude, or opinion is
   - (B) for explicit details or facts from the conversation to be identified
   - (C) about the organization of, or the relationship between two portions of, the conversation
   - (D) what the conversation is about or why the speakers are having the conversation

2. A lecture organization question asks
   - (A) about the relationship of ideas in a passage
   - (B) for explicit details or facts from the lecture to be identified
   - (C) what the lecture is about or why it is being given
   - (D) about the organization of, or the relationship between two portions of, the lecture

Key Vocabulary Practice

B. Fill in the blanks with the correct words.

roommates	part-time	job	model	split	transportation

1. The Burgess model uses circles to _____ the city into different areas.

2. Many people use public _____ to travel around their cities.

3. Many students have _____ jobs because they only have a limited amount of time.

4. Dorm rooms often have to be shared between two or more _____.

5. To make money most people have a _____ they go to every day.

6. Burgess is famous for his _____ that explains how cities develop.

[12] Conversation

Getting Ready to Listen

A. Learn the words.

Key Vocabulary

geometry	a branch of mathematics concerned with angles, measurement, and figures in space
tricky	not easy to do
volunteer	a person who offers to do something; a person who works without pay

TOEFL® Vocabulary

program	a plan of action to accomplish a goal
discouraged	feeling hopeless about something
practice	to do something over and over again to improve the skill
formula	a specific set of steps for doing something
afford	to have enough money to buy or pay for something

B. Learn the question type.

TOEFL® Question Type

Content

What is the likely outcome of doing X then Y?

What can be inferred about X?

Indicate whether each of the following was mentioned in the conversation.

- This type of question is asking about the relationship of ideas in the conversation.
- The answer may include ideas that have been stated or implied.
- The question may include a table for information to be organized into.

Practice

A. **Listen to the first part of the conversation and choose the correct answers.**
Track 2-49

1. What is the main topic of this conversation?

   (A) A student's request for help   (B) A math teacher's methods

2. How does the student explain the problem?

   (A) He says the teacher's math review was not clear enough.

   (B) He says he had problems with the questions.

Note-taking

B. **Listen to the full conversation and take notes.** Track 2-50

Man - Student	Woman - Professor
• Is _____ • Failed the _____ _____ • Thinks that _____ • Can't _____	• Knows a couple of things he can do: _____ • Geometry can be _____ • Don't get _____ • Can stay after _____ _____ • Going over the _____ • New tutoring program is _____ _____ • Volunteers help _____ _____ _____

C. Choose the correct answers.

1. Why did the professor mention extra practice?

(A) To show him that all the things she mentioned are good

(B) To show that he doesn't need to do anything that she mentioned

2. What is the likely outcome of the student reviewing more and then taking a math test?

(A) He will get better grades on the next test.

(B) He will be able to tutor other classmates.

3. Indicate whether each of the following was mentioned in the conversation. Place a checkmark in the True or False column.

Statement	True	False
The student failed the test.		
Geometry is easy.		
The tutoring program is too expensive.		

TOEFL® Vocabulary Practice

D. Fill in the blanks with the correct words.

program	discouraged	practice	formula	afford

1. There is often a special _____ for solving difficult math questions.

2. A student will often feel _____ if they can't understand the teacher.

3. People who want to lose weight often start an exercise _____.

4. Athletes usually _____ often.

5. Many parents wonder how they will _____ to pay for their children's university tuition.

Test

🎧 Listen to the conversation and take notes. `Track 2-51`

Woman - Student	Man - Professor
• Didn't do well on _____ _____	• Can meet at _____ _____ _____
• Always been good at _____ _____	
• Used to be a _____ _____ _____ _____ _____ _____ _____ _____ _____	• Asks if reviews _____ _____ _____ _____ _____ _____ _____

Choose the correct answers. `Track 2-52`

1. Why is the woman speaking to the man?

(A) She wants to arrange a time to meet.
(B) She wants to say goodbye before he leaves.
(C) He asked to speak with her for a few minutes.
(D) He set up an appointment to go over her test.

2. What is the man doing?

(A) Teaching a class   (B) Grading the woman's test
(C) Leaving for the day   (D) Tutoring a student

3. What is the opinion of the man when he says this: 🎧 ?

(A) He believes the material is easy.
(B) He is confident she will get better.
(C) He thinks the woman won't pass the class.
(D) He feels the woman does not need any extra help with math.

4. What can be inferred about the woman?

(A) She dislikes geometry.   (B) She dislikes the teacher.
(C) She cares about her math grade. (D) She has never been good at math.

Lecture - Music

Getting Ready to Listen

A. Learn the words.

Key Vocabulary

record	to copy sounds or images onto a machine that can play them back
microphone	a device that captures sound to either record or project
notice	to have something catch one's attention

TOEFL® Vocabulary

equipment	tools and machines that help with specific tasks
recognize	to know something from hearing or seeing it before
interfere	to get in the way of something
session	an amount of time spent doing a specific activity
separate	to set or keep apart from something else

B. Learn the question type.

TOEFL® Question Type

Content

What is the likely outcome/was the outcome of doing X then Y?

What can be inferred about X?

Indicate whether each of the following was mentioned in the lecture.

- This type of question is asking about the relationship of ideas in the lecture.
- The answer may include ideas that have been stated or implied.
- The question may include a table for information to be organized into.

Practice

A. **Listen to the first part of the lecture and choose the correct answers.**

Track 2-53

1. What is the main topic of this lecture?

   (A) Recording equipment
   (B) How musical styles are different

2. What are the key points in this lecture?

   (A) The invention of recording equipment caused music to sound different.
   (B) Vibrato has become the most popular musical style for string instruments.

3. How does the professor describe the main topic?

   (A) By comparing recording equipment with other inventions
   (B) By showing a cause and effect of recording equipment

4. Choose the best note-taking diagram for this lecture.

   (A) Problem and Solution
   Diagram
   (B) Cause Effect
   Diagram
   (C) Ordering Diagram

Note-taking

B. **Draw the diagram chosen in question 4. Then insert the information from questions 1 and 2.**

C. **Now listen to the full lecture and complete your notes.** Track 2-54

D. Choose the correct answers.

1. What can be inferred about vibrato before recording equipment was invented?

    (A) It wasn't used often.

    (B) It was only used by drums.

2. What was the outcome of using vibrato during recordings?

    (A) The instruments could be heard better

    (B) Violin music became more popular

3. What is the professor's opinion of recording equipment?

    (A) He thinks it is amazing that it changed music.

    (B) He thinks it shouldn't have changed music.

TOEFL® Vocabulary Practice

E. Fill in the blanks with the correct words.

recognized	equipment	separate	interfere	session

1. The sounds of certain musical instruments can _____ with the sound of other instruments.

2. Modern recording equipment can _____ the different sounds in music.

3. Famous musicians are _____ all over the world.

4. Most recording _____ is very sensitive and expensive.

5. A recording _____ can last for a few hours or last all day.

Test

Listen to the lecture and take notes. `Track 2-55`

Duke Ellington

- Played on Radio

- Wrote and Recorded Own Music

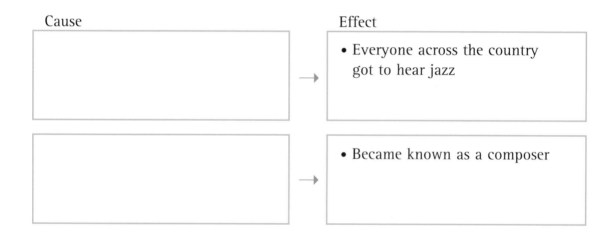

Cause

Effect

- Everyone across the country got to hear jazz

→

- Became known as a composer

→

Choose the correct answers. `Track 2-56`

1. What is the main idea of the lecture?

(A) How a musician made jazz popular in the US
(B) The history of jazz music in the US
(C) How Duke Ellington started in the music business
(D) How Duke Ellington taught his style to other musicians

2. Why does the professor mention national radio?

 (A) To show how live music was becoming less popular
 (B) To explain the importance of having jazz played on it
 (C) To describe the differences between national and local radio
 (D) To suggest that musicians preferred live music to radio

3. What is the professor's attitude towards live music?

 (A) He does not like it.
 (B) He thinks it made jazz music popular.
 (C) He does not think it was as effective as the radio in getting new people to listen.
 (D) He thinks that live music is much better than the radio.

4. According to the professor, what effect did Ellington have on the way people viewed jazz?

 (A) He made the music popular in the US.
 (B) People started comparing it to blues music.
 (C) More people became composers.
 (D) People thought jazz as boring.

Listen again to part of the lecture. Then answer the question.

5. Why does the professor say this: ?

 (A) To show how hard other musicians worked
 (B) To emphasize how effective the other musicians were
 (C) To give an example of how popular Jazz music was
 (D) To emphasize that Duke was doing something different

6. What does the professor imply about jazz before Ellington?

 (A) No one played it as well as he did.
 (B) People were not very impressed with it.
 (C) It was only played in certain parts of the US.
 (D) They did not teach it in musical schools.

Check-up

A. Choose the correct answers.

1. A conversation content question asks

   (A) what the speaker's emotion, attitude, or opinion is
   (B) for explicit details or facts from the conversation to be identified
   (C) about the relationship of ideas in a conversation
   (D) why the speaker has said something

2. A lecture content question asks

   (A) what the lecture is about or why it is being given
   (B) what the speaker's emotion, attitude, or opinion is
   (C) why the speaker has said something
   (D) about the relationship of ideas in a lecture

Key Vocabulary Practice

B. Fill in the blanks with the correct words.

record	microphone	notice	geometry
tricky	volunteer		

1. The lead singer in a band usually uses a _____.

2. Studying _____ is how children learn about shapes.

3. Big changes are easy to _____.

4. Learning how to tie and untie the knots used on sailboats can be _____.

5. It is often hard to _____ the music played by softer sounding instruments in an orchestra.

6. A _____ is someone who freely gives their time to help in ways that make a difference to others.

[Review 2]

Review 2   145

Conversation 1

🎧 Listen to the conversation and take notes.   Track 2-57

Woman - Student	Man - Professor

• Failed _____
 • Spent a lot of _____
  _____
 • One member kept _____
 _____
 _____
 _____
 _____
 _____
	• Liked their theme but ____
	  _____
	 • If they expanded _____
	  _____
	  _____
	  _____
	  _____
	  _____

Choose the correct answers.   Track 2-58

1. What are the speakers mainly discussing?

(A) A lazy student   (B) A recent test
(C) An upcoming project   (D) Grades

2. Which of the following problems with the group member does the student NOT mention?

(A) Interrupted other group members   (B) Didn't work hard
(C) Was always late for group meetings (D) Interfered with the group's work

3. Why does the professor mention the "real world"?

(A) To explain why the group failed the project
(B) To prepare the group for the next project
(C) To make the point that you don't always get to choose who you work with
(D) To help the students improve their grades

4. What is the professor's opinion of the student's problem?

(A) That the complaint is valid, and he will change the grade
(B) He will not assign any more group projects
(C) He will fail only the lazy student
(D) That they had a chance to solve the problem, but now it is too late

Lecture 1

🎧 **Listen to the lecture and take notes.** Track 2-59

Saving the Environment

- Recycle

- Elect strong leaders

- New methods

The Environment

- Get rid of extra waste

- A good plan for clean air

- Get rid of harmful substances

Choose the correct answers. Track 2-60

1. What is the lecture mainly about?

(A) Special equipment
(B) Recycling programs
(C) The environment
(D) Strong leaders

2. Why does the professor say this: ( ) ?

    (A) To explain that the world was cleaner twenty years ago
    (B) To show that the environment is healthy
    (C) To show that more needs to be done to protect the environment
    (D) To show that it is easy to clean up the environment

3. How does recycling help the environment?

    (A) It helps to get rid of waste.
    (B) Recycling plants make the air clean.
    (C) Less people will use dangerous chemicals.
    (D) It makes rivers and lakes cleaner.

4. Why does the professor say this: ( ) ?

    (A) No one believes that the environment is in danger
    (B) To show that politicians should be the ones to take action
    (C) To show that a clean planet is everyone's responsibility
    (D) To show that a clean planet is good for you

5. What can be inferred about electing strong leaders when it comes to the environment?

    (A) Strong leaders can carry more garbage.
    (B) Strong leaders have the power to make useful laws to protect the environment.
    (C) Strong leaders produce less garbage than other people.
    (D) Strong leaders can invent new machines to clean up garbage.

6. Why does the professor mention cleaner vehicles?

    (A) We need vehicles to carry garbage to recycling plants.
    (B) Vehicles are a major source of pollution.
    (C) Everyone should have a vehicle.
    (D) Driving a car is better for the environment than taking a bus.

🎧 **Listen to the lecture and take notes.** `Track 2-61`

Bird Flu

- Symptoms
  - similar to regular flu

- See Doctor
  - will perform examination

- Treatment
  - same drugs as regular flu

Symptoms		See Doctor		Treatment

Choose the correct answers. `Track 2-62`

1. What is the lecture mainly about?

(A) Regular flu   (B) Birds

(C) Bird flu   (D) Doctors

2. According to the professor, which is NOT a symptom of bird flu?

(A) Bleeding gums   (B) Cough

(C) Fever   (D) Muscle aches

3. Why does the professor say this: ◯ ?

    (A) To show that the regular flu is much more dangerous than bird flu

    (B) To encourage the students not to eat chicken

    (C) To scare the students

    (D) To show how dangerous bird flu is

4. What is the professor's opinion on bird flu symptoms?

    (A) You should wait and see if they go away by themselves

    (B) You should see your doctor right away

    (C) You should eat chicken soup and get some rest

    (D) You should eat healthy foods and get a lot of exercise

5. Why does the professor mention that you should see your doctor right away if you think you have the flu?

    (A) To show that people don't need to worry about catching bird flu

    (B) To show that quick treatment is very important

    (C) To show that the bird flu is harmless

    (D) To show that only birds can catch the bird flu

6. What can be inferred about medical research?

    (A) It is easy.

    (B) It is cheap.

    (C) It can take a long time to find results.

    (D) Most universities are not interested in medical research.

Lecture 3

Listen to the lecture and take notes. **Track 2-63**

Oil Spill in Alaska

- Killed many animals

- Hurt economy

- New machine invented

Cause	Effect
• Large ship sank	
• Clean up not quick	
• New grooved oil skimmer made	
• Countries lend oil skimmers	

Choose the correct answers. **Track 2-64**

1. What is the main idea of the lecture?

(A) More large ships are needed to carry oil

(B) New technology can help clean up oil spills

(C) Oil spills are a great danger to the environment

(D) Oil spills are bad for the economy

2. Why does the professor mention the oil spill off Alaska?

(A) To show that technology is unnecessary in cleaning up oil spills
(B) To show that no accidents have occurred since then
(C) To show the effects of an oil spill on the environment
(D) To show the similarities between the new skimmer and the old skimmer

3. What is the professor's attitude towards the new oil skimming invention?

(A) He thinks that it is a big improvement over the old system of skimming
(B) He believes that the new invention is unnecessary
(C) He doesn't think there will be any more oil spills
(D) He believes that this invention is all that is needed to keep the oceans clean

4. According to the professor, what effect did the oil spill in Alaska have on the local economy?

(A) It was helpful to the local economy
(B) It created jobs in the area where the oil spill occurred
(C) It had no effect on the local economy
(D) It was harmful to the local economy

5. Why does the professor say this: ( ) ?

(A) To show that helping each other is just as important as technology
(B) To show that other countries plan on having oil spills
(C) To show that countries do not wish to help each other
(D) To show that countries do not need oil skimmers

6. What does the professor imply about clean-up efforts during the oil spill off the Alaskan coast in 1989?

(A) The technology available back then was good
(B) There was only a small amount of oil spilled
(C) The US President was pleased with the efforts
(D) Skimmers in 1989 did not work as well as people had hoped

Conversation 2

🎧 **Listen to the conversation and take notes.** `Track 2-65`

Man - Student	Woman - University Employee
• Would like to change ____ _____ • Roommate never _____ _____ • Dirty dishes from _____ _____ _____ _____ _____ _____	• Asks if the roommate has _____ _____ _____ _____ _____ _____ _____ _____

Choose the correct answers. `Track 2-66`

1. What are the speakers mainly discussing?

    (A) A problem with the dorm room   (B) A problem with grades

    (C) A difficult roommate   (D) The cost of an apartment

2. Which of the following concerns about the roommate does the student NOT mention?

    (A) Being rude   (B) Coming home late

    (C) Messy   (D) Waking the student up

3. Why does the student say this: 🎧 ?

    (A) To get his roommate in trouble

    (B) To show that he has no more patience for his roommate

    (C) Because he hates his roommate

    (D) To show that his roommate is trying hard to change

4. Which information is true of the student and which is true of the student's roommate? For each phrase below, place a checkmark in the "Student" column or the "Roommate" column.

	Student	Roommate
Needs to improve his grades this session		
Doesn't clean up after himself		
Can't afford an off-campus apartment		
Comes home too late and makes noise		

Basic Skills for the TOEFL® iBT 1

Iain Donald Binns
Micah Sedillos

Listening

Transcript & Answer Key

Transcript

[Unit 1]

Conversation

Practice

W: Excuse me. Do you think you could show me how to get an ID for the computer lab? This is my first semester, so I don't have one yet. But all my professors said I'd need one. For example, I will need one in my science class tomorrow.

M: Sure, I can help you. Most freshman classes do need an ID and a password. (*Practice A end.*)

W: Why? I mean, can't we just leave the computers logged in all the time?

M: No. Passwords and stuff are too important. If you want privacy while you're using the computer, you have to have passwords. Otherwise, people could get into our computers and steal all our students' and staff's personal information.

W: OK, so how do I get an ID and a password?

M: Well, first you need to fill out a form. You need to put your name, address, and what you want your password to be. Then someone will put it into the computer for you. You should be able to use the computer in your class tomorrow.

W: That's great. Can you give me a form?

M: Sure, here you go.

W: That's great! Thanks for your help. Bye.

Test

W: OK, so you want to send an email. You've never done this before?

M: No, I haven't.

W: Well, you'll learn pretty fast. It's easy. By the end of the semester, you'll be really good at it. OK, do you have an ID and password?

M: Yes I do! I've already logged in.

W: Great! Ok now just use the mouse and put the arrow over this little picture. It will take you to the email system. Your professor in your freshman computing class will explain all about that.

M: [*Excitedly.*] Oh, actually, one of my friends explained it all to me the other day. It was pretty interesting.

W: Well, then, you already know a little bit about it. Now, just type the email address here and your message here. Also, you shouldn't send any personal information in your email.

M: Oh really? Why?

W: You have to be careful to protect your privacy.

M: Oh yeah, that's true. [*Pause.*] OK I have finished writing my email, what do I do now?

W: You just click on "send."

M: That's it?

W: Yeah, it's that easy!

M: Great! Thanks for your help.

W: You're welcome. Let me know if you have any other problems.

M: OK. I will.

Lecture

Practice

M: OK class. I want to talk to you about the Cold War today. Now, the Cold War wasn't just one single war. It was actually a long time of aggression. It, um, it lasted about fifty years! Anyway, the Cold War was mainly between the US and the USSR. That was Russia's old name. They had different opinions on just about everything. (*Practice A end.*) Oh, and Joseph Stalin, who we have talked about before, was the leader of the USSR at the start of the Cold War.

Anyway! There was a lot of suspicion during the Cold War. But, the US and the USSR never actually fought each other. This is because both countries had nuclear weapons. So, they were afraid of each other. They didn't want to destroy the whole world. And that might have happened... if they'd fought each other. But, instead of fighting, they showed their different opinions by competing with each other. For example, they made their militaries bigger. And they raced each other to see who could get a person in space first. Stuff like that. But, a lot of the problems were political. The two countries were very different, and so they couldn't get along. This is what caused the Cold War.

Test

W: OK, so we've been talking about the Cold War... Let's see. I'm going to tell you the three main ways that the two countries were "warring." Remember, the Cold War was mainly between the USSR and the USA. They had many political differences. Most of the Cold War was about competing with each other. Neither country wanted to, to... get beat. And I mean, in ANYTHING!

All right, so they had different opinions on many things. First, there was a lot of suspicion. And so they made their militaries bigger and bigger. I mentioned this before. They made a lot of weapons including nuclear weapons.

Another way that they were competing was in technology. They didn't want to fall behind. So, they were always spying on each other. They would steal each other's secrets.

M: Didn't you mention something about a space race the last time?

W: Yes, and that's the last big way they were competing---in the space race. This is just what it sounds like. The two countries were racing each other to be the first to send someone into space. Uh, the USSR won. They were first to send someone into space. But, the U.S. was the first to send someone to the moon.

And that's it. That's the Cold War. There were some very scary times, though. The two countries had a lot of aggression and there were many moments that could've been really dangerous. They could have even destroyed each other!

[Unit 2]

Conversation

Practice

M: Hi, I need to find some books for my chemistry class.
W: Sure, what do you need?
M: Here's my list.
W: Oh, are you in Professor Jenkins's class?
M: Yes I am.
W: She sent us an email to say that she has revised the lists for a few of her classes. Do you have the updated list? (*Practice A end.*)
M: Uh, what do you mean updated list?
W: Well, she actually replaced some of the books with different ones.
M: I really need that new list. How can I get it?
W: If you know the course number, I can tell you if your class's book list has changed.
M: Hmmm, I don't think I can remember it.
W: Well, you can pick up the list at the professor's office. Do you know where her office is?
M: Yeah. But it's quite far away. I'll have to walk across campus to her office.
W: You could go online and look up the course number and then I could tell you the books you need. The computer lab is quite close!
M: Yeah, and I know that the computer lab is open. Hmm... I think I'll go there. Thanks for your help!

Test

W: Hey Mr. Daniels, I saw the bookstore's online update. Did you get the chemistry books in?
M: Hi Amy. Yes, our store just got them today.
W: Oh, great! Actually, do you have used copies of any of them?
M: Oh, I'm sorry, right now we don't.

W: That's too bad. I really wanted a used copy.

M: Well, can you wait another couple of days?

W: Maybe. You see I'm running a little low on money.

M: Yeah, the used books are cheaper. But, do you really want a book that's already been written on?

W: No, I suppose not.

M: Also, if you wait for a used book you won't be able to start studying for your courses immediately.

W: Yeah. You're right... I'd only save a couple of dollars anyway. I'll just need to try to revise what I spend my money on. Try to save a little more.

M: That's a good idea. And, you know what? If you're running low on money, we could use someone to work here at the campus bookstore. And the computer lab next door needs someone too!

W: Really? That's a great idea! I am not very good with computers though, I don't even send emails! But I'll think about working here! Thanks!

Lecture

Practice

W: Let's talk about art called Neo-Impressionism. Neo means new. So, Neo-Impressionism means new Impressionism. This was the new art back in the 1880s. But, um, it wasn't just new. It was different too. Georges Seurat invented this new art. He used a precise way of painting. And, well, it was different from any other art of the time. So, let's look at how these old and new styles were different. (*Practice A end.*)

Although most artists used people and nature, most artists of this time didn't plan their paintings. They didn't have people pose. They didn't arrange scenes. However, these new paintings were planned in an exact way. This was the first difference.

Now the second difference was using pure color. Most artists mixed their paints together. This made various colors. But these new artists didn't mix any colors at all. So, they both used paint but they used it in different ways.

The artists used their paintbrushes in different ways too. This was the biggest difference. Most artists painted in brush strokes. OK? But Seurat didn't. He painted in tiny dots. This took a long time. A very long time!

The purpose of this new art was to represent people and nature in a true way. These new artists felt their paintings reproduced life in a way that seemed more real.

Test

M: OK, yesterday we read about Georges Seurat. Now, many people would like to paint like Seurat. But, very few people can. He invented a very precise way of painting. It looks different and is hard to do because it is so exact. There were various styles of painting but Seurat decided to make a different one.

The first difference was that Seurat took a lot of time to prepare before he painted. He planned his paintings very carefully. He made many drawings to decide on the best way to reproduce the scene. He worked for many hours before he started to paint. With this style, you have to have a clear purpose. With other styles at this time, they had very little time to prepare.

Now, the second difference was that he used pure colors. He understood that the eye would blend the colors. He knew if he painted red next to yellow, the eye would see orange. OK?

W: Why didn't he just mix the paints like other artists? Wouldn't that have been easier?

M: Yes, but using pure colors made the painting very bright. These paintings don't look bright in books. But when you see them in person. Wow! They are great!

Now, as you know the biggest difference was that Seurat didn't use brush strokes. He painted tiny dots. One at a time. Millions and millions of dots and some of his paintings were VERY big! Can you imagine how long this took? One painting took two years! Of course, that didn't mean that Seurat was a better painter. All the well-known painters back then were very good and made beautiful paintings. But, Seurat was very proud of his different way of painting. He felt that this new style represented people and nature very well.

Transcript

[Unit 3]

Conversation

Practice

M: Hi, Professor Smith. Do you have a few minutes?

W: Sure. How can I help?

M: I want to know how to write a good essay.

W: I see. What exactly is the problem?

M: Well, I'm not sure. I mean I take many notes, and I understand the lessons. It's just that my essays aren't very good.

W: Ah, yes. A good essay needs organization. Let's go over the format for an essay. (*Practice A end.*)

M: That'd be great.

W: So there are the three parts to an essay. First, there's the introduction. You need a strong introduction. This gives the main idea for your whole essay. OK?

M: That makes sense.

W: Next, there are the body paragraphs. They provide evidence or details for your main idea.

M: OK. [*Slowly.*] I think I should write this down.

W: Yes, that is a good idea.

M: OK. [*Quickly.*] Can you tell me about body paragraphs again?

W: Sure. The body paragraphs provide evidence or details.

M: Ahhh right.

W: And then there's your conclusion. The conclusion is just a summary of your main idea.

M: Wow! I've never thought of it that way.

W: Yes, it can make a big difference. Good organization is important for essay writing.

Test

W: Hi, Professor Johnson. Can I talk to you?

M: Why, yes, Carrie.

W: Oh, great! I need some help with my essay. I'm having problems finding good information other than the things from the lessons. And I'm not very good at taking notes.

M: Hmm... OK. Let's talk about finding good information first. Books are the best. But, these days, you can look online too.

W: OK. How do I decide what websites and books to use?

M: Well, with the Internet, you type in a subject and you'll get a list of websites. With books, do a search on the library computer. It will give a list of useful books. It's very easy.

W: Wow. That is easy. OK, then what?

M: Take notes. Don't copy everything. You only need a summary of the information. With books, sometimes reading the introduction and conclusion first will help you to decide if it is useful.

W: Yeah, I've been reading a lot. And I always copy down too much.

M: Just take notes that will give you the evidence you need for your essay paragraphs. Oh, and the organization of your notes is important too. You will have to find your information again easily.

W: Right. Of course. Thanks so much for your help!

Lecture

Practice

M: The winter can be a problem for some animals. Why? Because the extreme cold can kill them. So do you know what some creatures do to solve this problem? They hibernate. They go into a deep sleep. Today we will talk about bats; what problems they have in winter and how they solve these.

Bats hibernate for two reasons. First, it is cold, so they do it to stay warm. And second, they do it because it's hard to find food in the winter. As a result, they can survive the winter. (*Practice A end.*)

The winter is very bad for bats. They're sensitive to the cold. The average bat can't live through the winter by itself. So, they have a special way to solve this problem. Bats sleep together. They go into places like caves. Anywhere out of the cold. They shield each other from the cold. And they're able to make it through the winter.

Bats also hibernate during the winter because food is hard to find. Most bats eat insects. This is a problem. Why? Most insects disappear during the winter. They die or go underground. So bats must eat more food than usual during the fall. Then, they live off their body fat while they hibernate. This way they can survive until the insects come out again in the spring.

Test

W: Today, we're going to talk about snakes. Can you imagine eating a snake? Me neither. But there are creatures that do. This is a problem for snakes. So how do they solve this problem? They have to protect themselves. Let's look at three types of snakes. The rattlesnake, spitting cobra, and hognose snake. They all have unique ways of protecting themselves.

The rattlesnake solves this problem in a unique way. You see, rattlesnakes are born with small beads on their tails. As an average snake gets older, it grows more beads. These beads rub together and make a rattling sound. OK, so when does the rattlesnake make this noise? When it thinks an animal might attack it. It cannot shield itself so it tries to scare the creature by rattling its tail.

The spitting cobra has another way to protect itself. What does it do? It sprays poison from its mouth. OK? But this snake doesn't just spray it anywhere. No, it sprays it into the eyes of the creature that is attacking it. This is very effective because eyes are sensitive. The spray stops the creature from seeing. And the snake gets away.

Next, we have the hognose snake. It's less aggressive. So what does it do? The hognose snake plays dead. That's right! It will twist and roll like it's dying. Then it will lie still on its back. The snake will even hang its tongue out of its mouth! Can you believe that? So, by playing dead, it actually survives.

[Unit 4]

Conversation

Practice

W: Hi, Mr. Baker. Could you help me with something?
M: Sure. What can I do for you?
W: Well, I'd like to check out some library books. I have to do some research for an essay.
M: I see. Well, you've got two choices. You can either use the self-service machine, or you can take the books to the front desk. (*Practice A end.*)
W: Could you explain them both, please?
M: OK, sure. See that machine that looks like a computer?
W: Yeah.
M: Well, that's the self-service machine. You'll have to scan your student ID card. Wait a second; did you set up a student library account yet?
W: Yes.
M: OK, good. Anyway, then you scan the books, and the machine will print you a receipt. The receipt tells you when the books are due back.
W: Oh, that's great. I always forget when my books are due back.
M: Yeah. Just be sure to press your ID and the books on the scanner; it's sensitive sometimes.
W: OK, so what's my other checkout choice?
M: You can take your books over to the front desk, where the librarian will help you.
W: Oh, that's it? That's easy. Thanks for the help.

Test

W: Hello. Do you need help?

M: Hi. Yes, I'm doing research for my history essay and I'm trying to find a book, but I'm not sure where to begin.

W: No problem. Let's see... there are two ways to find books here. You can either use the computer system, or you can use the book lists.

M: How do the book lists work?

W: Well, the lists organize the books by their subjects. You're looking for a book on history. So, first you look under "History" on the list. Then you look at the title. Each book is in alphabetical order.

M: OK, I see.

W: Good. Each book has a number next to it, and those numbers tell you where to find that book.

M: I see. And did you mention something about a computer?

W: Oh yeah, I almost forgot. The computer is just as easy. Do a search for your book, and it will tell you where to find it.

M: Great! I should be able to find what I need. Thanks!

W: Oh, and remember if you want to check out any books you need to scan your ID card at the self-service machine. If you have any books due on your account, you won't be able to check out anymore.

M: OK, got it.

Lecture

Practice

W: OK, let's begin our study of light today. We all know what light is, of course. But today's lecture is about two properties of light. These properties are reflection and refraction. I'll repeat them. Reflection and refraction. (*Practice A end.*)

First, let's talk about reflection. It's easy to understand. Reflection happens when rays of light fall on a surface. The surface bounces these rays back up. When our eyes see this it is called reflection. A mirror is a great example. Right? Mirrors are so smooth that they reflect almost all the light rays that fall on them.

Next, let me explain refraction. Remember, light rays travel in lines. Straight lines, really. But things get in the way. Sometimes light has to pass through different materials. Then what do the light rays do? They bend. And, well, they go in a new direction. Now the light can move in a straight line again.

OK. Picture this. If you put a straw in a glass of water, the straw looks like it's broken in two. This is because the light rays bend when they meet the water. It looks like you have one straw above the water and a different straw under the water. All because of refraction.

Test

M: All right. Today's lecture is about heat. Actually, we will talk about the ways heat moves. This is called heat transfer. Now, there are three types of heat transfer. They are called [*slowly*] convection..., conduction..., and... radiation. OK?

OK! Convection happens when heat moves through gases and liquids. When air or water heat up, they get lighter. Then they move away from the heat. They rise. When they get cooler, they change direction. They come back down to the heat again. In convection, this repeats over and over. For example, a hot-air balloon. Fire heats the air. The hot air becomes lighter. The balloon rises up. But, as the air cools, it gets heavier. So, the balloon goes down. Convection is how hot-air balloons fly.

Now, next is conduction. This happens when heat moves through solids. First, a solid object is put on heat. Eventually the solid object takes this heat and it gets hot. Some materials are very good at conduction. Metals, for example. This is why many cooking pans are made of metal. They heat up quickly. But don't touch them. Ouch! Conduction causes many burns.

Finally, heat also moves by radiation. If you can feel heat from an object without touching it then it is radiating heat. Remember you can't see this heat. The sun, a toaster, a dryer. All these things use radiation. Have you ever warmed your hands by a fire? Even this is radiation. OK? Do we understand?

[Unit 5]

Conversation

Practice

M: Hi. Are you in charge of the Student Tutoring Center?
W: No, but I do tutor here.
M: Well, I need help with my mathematics class work. Can you help me?
W: That's fine. I'm actually a math major. I can help you. But, before we begin, I need to clarify the rules.
M: Rules? What rules?
W: Well, there are some things I can help you with, and some things I can't help you with. Let me explain. (*Practice A end.*)
M: OK.
W: First of all, our school has rules about cheating. It's pretty standard for schools nowadays. Anyway, according to the rules, if you cheat, then you can get kicked out of school.
M: That makes sense. I don't want them to punish either one of us because of tutoring.
W: Exactly. OK, so I can help you with things like learning strategies for studying, and studying from your notes. I can even help you take notes. However, when it comes to class work and homework, you're on your own. Are we all clear?
M: I think that's fair.
W: Good. OK, let's get started.

Test

W: Hi, Jim. I'm having some problems in class.
M: Well, that's why I tutor you. Are we talking about problems in mathematics class?
W: Yeah. I don't understand the professor's comments on my homework.
M: OK. Do you know why you might be having trouble with the work?
W: Not really.
M: Well, let's see if we can decide on some strategies.
W: Fine with me.
M: This type of thing is pretty standard. I've seen it many times. It's usually one or two things that can be fixed. For example, have you been going to all the lectures?
W: Well, not really. I'm not a math major or anything.
M: But if you don't go to lectures, how do you expect to understand the work? So that part is easily solved. How about the extra math exercises? Have you done them?
W: Um, no. Why would I do even MORE math work?
M: Well, you should, it will help you. <u>Let me clarify</u>... it will help you understand the basic lessons. I'm not going to punish you for coming here unprepared. I mean, you pay me to tutor you. But, you're only cheating yourself by not doing everything you can.
W: I know. You're right. I need to prepare more for this.
M: OK, let's begin.

Lecture

Practice

M: I want to tell you about advertising. Advertising is used to promote a product. Today we are going to look at billboard adverts. They use pictures to attract your attention. The picture that you see in an ad is the final step of a process. Before the billboard is made, a couple of things have to happen. First, the advertisers have to know the product. Then decide on a focus for the ad. Then they have to choose the right picture for it. (*Practice A end.*)

OK, like I said, the first step in making a billboard ad is to know the product. What does it do? Why buy it? Who buys it? Simple, huh? Well, the next step is to decide on its focus. This means that you have to choose what you want the ad to do. Usually you want the ad to get the customer to buy your product.

Next, you have to choose a picture for the ad. The picture has to look good. And it has to support the ad's focus. The milk billboard near the school is a good example. What's its focus? To have people drink more milk. And how does it do this? It shows a picture of a famous person drinking milk. It makes people want to drink more milk. So, the advert helps the product sell more.

Test

W: Ever heard of the "Four P's?" It's a marketing process. It's the process of a product. Using the Four P's can increase sales. They are [*slowly*] product..., price..., place..., and promotion. Let me explain.

The first step is to make a product. It's what a company tries to sell to its customers. This is important! For example, if we want to sell computer games. The product is a game. We have to make a game first. So, we study the games people already buy. We also study our potential customers. Then, we make a new game.

The next step is deciding on a price. The price should be low enough that people will buy the game but high enough so that we make money. We'll look at what other companies charge for their games. We'll look at how much people want to spend. Then we'll decide on the price.

The third step is finding a place to sell the product. The place has to be where our customers will go. Will we sell them in a store? Yes, Tom?

M: Let's sell them online. That's where I buy mine.

W: OK! We can sell them online. In fact, let's focus on selling them in a couple of places. Online and in computer stores.

The last step is promotion. This is usually advertising. It's what a company does to get customers to buy their product. Maybe we'll advertise on TV, on billboards, in a magazine, online. Anywhere we can attract people's attention.

[Unit 6]

Conversation

Practice

M: Hi. Can I help you with anything?
W: Hi, Professor. Well, it's about our project that's due next week. I was wondering if I could get an extension. Can I get an extra week to do it?
M: Why are you asking?
W: I normally wouldn't, but I've been really sick and I was absent for a few of your lectures.
M: Well, I'm sorry but I can't give you an extension. However, I can suggest a couple of ways to make up for lost time. (*Practice A end.*)
W: I hope so. I really need a good grade or I could lose my scholarship. Then I wouldn't be able to pay my tuition.
M: You'll be fine. Here's what you can do: borrow one of your classmate's notes from the lectures that you missed. Ask if he or she can help explain them to you.
W: OK.
M: Or you can go to the library and do the research yourself. I can give you an outline of the lectures that you missed. You can look up the main information. Either way, you should be fine.
W: Yeah, I guess you're right. I should get started. Thanks.

Test

M: Hi, Professor Smith. I'm having a problem with a classmate, and I'd like to talk about it.
W: OK, Matt, what's up?
M: Well, the problem is that my partner for the project isn't doing his work. He's absent most of the time.
W: Hmmm... that's not good.

M: Yeah, I think we're going to need an extension. Even though I have done all my work AND given him an outline of what he should do.

W: Yes, I understand that is a problem.

M: I'm really upset about this. My grades are important. I need to do well in order to keep my scholarship, or I can't pay my tuition. What can I do?

W: Well, I can help you out. After all, I am very happy with all of the tutoring work you've been doing.

M: Really? That would be great.

W: OK, you have two choices. The first is that I can tell your partner to work harder, or I can give you a new partner. What do you think?

M: How about I just change partners?

W: That's fine. Give me a day, and I'll let you know who it is.

M: Super! Thanks so much.

Lecture

Practice

W: OK. We've learned Global Warming is the rise of the Earth's temperatures. We also know it may be caused by pollution. But pollution isn't the only thing. There's proof that cosmic rays can also affect the Earth's temperature. Let me explain.

First, what are cosmic rays? Well, they're energy from the sun. But how does that affect us on Earth? Well, they affect our clouds. (*Practice A end.*) In fact, they make clouds. You see, when these rays hit the Earth, they break into tiny electrical particles. These particles stay in the air. And, they attract water from the air. This water gathers in groups, and makes what? Clouds! Yes, clouds are formed.

Clouds are important. They bounce heat from the sun back into space. So, when there are more clouds, the Earth is cooler. OK, erm. Ahh yes... Remember I said that cosmic rays affect the temperatures? Well, scientists think there are fewer of these rays. Fewer cosmic rays mean fewer clouds. And fewer clouds mean higher temperatures! See? So that, along with pollution, may have caused the recent rise in the Earth's temperature.

Test

M: A little thing can have a big effect. Take space junk, for example. Things that we send into space, such as satellites and shuttles, leave small particles of metal, screws, and even paint behind. This junk floats in space around the Earth. And guess what? It's very dangerous. But don't worry... it's no harm to us on the Earth. But for the people in space shuttles, it's a matter of life and death. Let me explain.

Why is space junk dangerous to space shuttles? Well, the junk orbits the Earth. And when something orbits the Earth, it moves very fast, about 7,700 meters per second! So, even something small can affect the shuttles in a bad way.

W: Wait a second. That can't be true!

M: You want proof? Well, one shuttle got a dent a couple of inches deep. What do you think caused this? A tiny piece of paint! As a result, stronger materials are used on the outside of shuttles. So if a shuttle gets hit by space junk, it won't do as much damage.

But that's not all. Shuttles now move differently. The important equipment is near the front of the shuttle. If this gets harmed by space junk, then the shuttle may not be able to return to Earth. So to protect it, shuttles now orbit the Earth backwards. Clever, huh?

Transcript

[Review 1]

Conversation 1

[*Knock on door.*]
W: Come in!
M: Hi, Dr. White. My name is James. I'm in your Chemistry class.
W: Hi, James. Have a seat.
M: Thank you.
W: What can I do for you?
M: Well, I've missed a lot of classes. I had a cold.
W: Do you have a doctor's note?
M: Yes, right here.
W: Good. I'm glad you came to see me. So you need some help with the material you missed?
M: Err... yeah.
W: Okay, let me see. Each day I give students a handout. It contains a summary of the lecture. I can give you those. Can you tell me what classes you missed?
M: Sure. I've missed every class for the past two weeks.
W: Okay. Here you go. But the summaries aren't enough. You should get lecture notes from your classmates. Do you know anyone in the class?
M: Err... yeah... I think so. There's one girl who lives near me.
W: Great. Let me know if you can't get the notes.
M: Okay, I will.
W: And remember—I'm always here during my office hours. If you have any problems come and see me. I can clarify anything that might be confusing.
M: Okay. Thank you very much.

Lecture 1

W: OK. So, Impressionism was a new way of painting. It went against old art standards. It changed what was seen as good art. Before it, art was considered good if it was exact. Artists tried to reproduce what they saw on the canvas. They aimed to make the painting look just like what they could see. Impressionist painters were different.

The first thing you will notice in an Impressionist painting is the use of color. These artists didn't mix colors. They put two colors side by side. They knew the eyes would blend the colors for them. The purpose was to create bright and bold colors.

Movement was also important. Painters often worked outdoors. This was not normal at the time. Most painters had someone pose for them inside. But the Impressionist went outside. First, they wanted to capture life as it was happening. Their subjects were doing something. They were not posing. Blurred lines showed movement.

They paid attention to lighting. Working outside allowed artists to use natural light. This is always changing. The change comes through in the painting. Different times of year are represented with the change in seasons.

Impressionist Art changed art. It broke the rules. Many people did not like it for this reason. If you ask me, that's what makes it so great. And over time, many people agreed.

Lecture 2

M: OK. Today we are going to talk about bears. What is a bear?

W: It's a creature with fur, four legs, and paws. It has small ears and a long nose.

M: Good. What else?

W: It's very dangerous.

M: Oh? Even panda bears?

W: Oh, no. They're not dangerous. They're peaceful.

M: That's right. Other bears are hunters. But panda bears usually eat plants. So, they are not usually dangerous. Unless... their babies are near. That's when bears are really dangerous. Even pandas. All bears want to protect their young. So, they are sensitive and will get very violent. A similarity then is that pandas and bears are dangerous when they are protecting their babies. But! Pandas are usually not dangerous unlike other bears.

OK, more differences. Most bears live alone, but there is some evidence to suggest that some pandas actually do live in small groups. Another big difference is that pandas do not hibernate in the winter. Other bears do.

The last difference is that many pandas are going extinct. That means that there may be no more pandas left. They might ALL die. The main cause of this is that they are losing their homes. When we cut down forests, then pandas lose their homes. Also, they don't have many babies. Also, there are people who hunt them. Of course, all bears are hunted. But all of these factors affect panda bears more. So, more pandas are dying than are being born.

Lecture 3

W: Welcome to Physics 101. I'm sure you're all excited to learn.

[*Students groan.*]

W: Oh, you think physics is boring? A waste of time? Think about it, though, physics is very useful. It has helped solve various major problems. Take electricity. Before that, everything stopped when the sun went down. Now we can do business all night. It's changed our lives. What other problems has Physics solved?

M: Well, using oil to heat our homes is not clean. But nuclear power is. It doesn't pollute the air.

W: That's right! But it can be dangerous. What about nuclear weapons? At times, when we solve one problem, we create another. What else? How has physics made our lives easier?

M: Um... microwaves?

W: Yes, microwaves. Microwave ovens are useful. Before them, it took a long time to heat up food. Now you can up the temperature in no time. This is great for people these days. We're all so busy. But how else have microwaves helped. And I don't just mean the microwaves that we cook food in. The waves are very useful.

M: I think they're used in TV. Not normal TV, but when we watch something live. Is that right?

W: Yes! They're good for news reporters. Like when they are in far away places. They can use them to send pictures. Before microwaves, it was difficult to send pictures far away. With microwaves, it's just more practical and we get to watch things faster! Well, I hope I've done a good job of promoting physics to you. See you next time.

Conversation 2

W: Hi, I'd like to borrow this book.
M: I'm sorry, but this is a reference book. You can't borrow it.
W: Why not? My professor said it would help me research my essay topic.
M: Yes, but you have to do that here. You can't take the book out of the library.
W: Oh really? Okay then. What about journal articles? Can I take those home?
M: No, I'm afraid not. There is a lot of demand for reference material. It wouldn't be fair to the other students.

W: Okay, so, how do I find journal articles?

M: First, you do a search on the Library Database. You can enter keywords, and it will give you a list of articles that suit your topic.

W: Then what?

M: Write them down and bring them to the reference section of the library. They will give you the journal. You just need to show proof that you are a student here.

W: Proof?

M: Yes, your student ID.

W: Oh, yes of course. What about regular books, like novels?

M: You can bring those here. I will scan the book and then you can take it home.

W: When are they due back?

M: For most books, you are allowed to borrow them for three weeks.

[Unit 7]

Conversation

Practice

W: Hi. Do you work here?

M: Yes, I do. What can I do for you?

W: Well, I'm a student here, and I want to use the sports center. What do I need to do?

M: Well, you need to do two things. You need to open an account, and you need to pay for a locker.

W: Can you tell me how to do both? (*Practice A end.*)

M: Sure. The account is easy. Just show me your student ID, and I'll print you a membership card. We're open to the public too, but students don't have to pay a membership fee.

W: That's great!

M: OK, next, the locker. People tend to get a locker at each visit but you can also pay to use one that's only yours. Also, when people do that we lend them a towel to use each time they visit.

W: That's nice because I don't want to have to bring my own towel. I think I will pay for a locker.

M: OK. Let me print your card and get your locker key. Oh, one more thing, if you want to use a court, then you have to reserve them.

W: Oh, ok.

M: That's everything!

W: Thanks very much.

Test

W: How can I help you today?

M: Well, I'd like to reserve a tennis court, but I don't know how to.

W: Well, there are two ways. First, do you have a gym membership?

M: Yes, I already have one.

W: Great, ok! The first way to reserve a court is in person. You can do that here at the front desk.

M: Are the courts often busy?

W: It really depends on the time of day. We are open to the public, so the mornings and evenings tend to be the busiest.

M: Right, makes sense.

W: But if you're worried about not being able to get a court in person, then you should call us before you come. That's the other way to reserve one.

M: OK, so I just call the front desk?

W: That's right. An employee will take your name and the time you'd like to use the court.

M: Hmm... that sounds like the best way. Oh, do I have to pay a fee to use the tennis court?

W: No, that's included in your membership. We will also lend you a tennis racket and balls.

M: Oh great! Also, where are the lockers?

W: Just down the hall. Anything else?

M: Nope, that's it. Thanks a lot.

Practice

M: We've been talking about bestsellers that had great impact on people. Well, today... we're going to discuss *The Catcher in the Rye*. It has sold more copies than *To Kill a Mockingbird*. This book is one of the most famous books of, um, of all time. It's about a young man who's trying to cope with growing up. He's a teenager whose life hasn't been very good.

There are three clear themes in the book. The main character, Holden, really criticizes people, he wants to protect younger people, and he has difficulty becoming an adult. (*Practice A end.*) His younger brother died some years earlier. This makes him angry and want to criticize people. It also makes him want to protect his younger sister from the hard parts of life. He doesn't want younger kids to experience the things he did. Finally, Holden is having a hard time becoming an adult. Um, he doesn't want to remain a kid. But he is having a hard time growing up. But he can't escape it. I mean, every teenager has problems. We all had problems growing up.

The Catcher in the Rye became a bestseller because people understand Holden's problems. Everyone has grown up, or will grow up. So everyone can find parts of themselves in this book.

Test

W: The book *Watership Down*... let's talk about it today. It has sold more than 50 million copies. This book's themes are people and politics. This book looks at how people treat each other and criticizes governments. It uses a story about rabbits. A group of rabbits leave home to find a new place to live. They can't remain in their old home because it's going to be destroyed. So, they escape.

After a while, the group finds a safe new home. But, they start fighting with other rabbit towns nearby. The rabbits in these towns are very different. And because of this, no one gets on. This shows how people in real life can't accept each other's differences.

One group of rabbits is called Efrafa. The leader is an adult male rabbit. He controls his town. He tells everyone what to do. No child, teenager, or adult has freedom to learn or experience anything there. The other group of rabbits is the Tharn Warren. It is also very bad. Things are too easy there. Growing up in a place like that means you learn very little.

Some people think that the two rabbit towns are like different kinds of governments in the world. And that no government is perfect.

M: Oh, I see! Having a really easy life is bad for you. This is like, uh, the Tharn Warren. The rabbits don't have to work to find food there. And Efrafa is a place where there is no real freedom. So it is bad too.

W: Yes, exactly. *Watership Down* may seem like a simple story about rabbits. But it asks real questions about how we live. This is why it is so popular.

[Unit 8]

Conversation

Practice

W: Hi. Are you the school's Activities Director?
M: Yes, I am. Can I help you?
W: Well, I just moved here, and I'd like to join a club.
M: OK, great! We have two types of clubs. The first type is sports and games. Additionally, we have community service clubs. First, you'll need to choose a club. Then you get a membership. (*Practice A end.*)
W: Do you have a chess club?
M: Yes, we do. Do you play?
W: Yes, I was president of my old school's chess club.

M: Oh really! I think that our chess club is going to elect new officers soon.
W: Sounds good, but I would like to do something different as well. What do the community service clubs do?
M: They usually help at local community centers. Members do things like tutor kids or help elderly people.
W: Oh, wow. It sounds like the clubs are really making a difference in the community. I would like to help.
M: That would be great! I think it's important for young people to learn how to help others.
W: So do I get my club membership here?
M: Yes, just let me get our forms.
W: Thanks!

Test

M: Hi Professor Johnson.
W: Hi Matt.
M: Don't you help in the chess club?
W: Yes, I do.
M: So who did they elect as the new president of the club?
W: It was very close, but Justin was elected.
M: Oh, cool. Anyway, I'm interested in joining a club as well, but I don't know which clubs we have at the school. I think a sports club would be best. Where can I find a list or something?
W: Well, you could look on the school website. Additionally, you could go to the sports office and check for information there.
M: Oh yeah? Where's the sports office?
W: It's right next to the health center.
M: OK, I know where that is. I'll go there after class, and if that doesn't work, then I'll just go to the computer lab and check online.
W: Sounds good.
M: So do you help with any other clubs?
W: Yes, I do.
M: Which one is it?
W: It's one of our school's community service clubs. We do things like help the elderly in our local area, and it's a lot of fun.
M: [*Uninspired.*] Yeah sounds great!
W: [*Laughing.*] It is!

Lecture

Practice

W: Today we're going to talk about what to do with our garbage. We make a lot of garbage, right? OK. So, what should we do with it? Well, we can do one or two things. First, we can put the garbage in landfills. Landfills are huge holes in the ground. And second, we can recycle our garbage. Let's compare these two methods, OK? (*Practice A end.*)

There are similarities between the use of landfills and recycling. For one thing, these are both ways to deal with waste products... things like used cans, bottles, newspapers, etc. All these things can either be thrown into a landfill or recycled. In many cities, it costs almost the same to put all this waste in landfills as it does to recycle it.

So now, let's look at the differences between landfills and recycling. When we put garbage in landfills, it just sits there. When we recycle it, we actually reuse it. So this is an important difference. You see, landfills take up a lot of space. And there is not much space. Recycling actually reuses waste products. It is also better for the environment. I'd say it's a good method compared to just throwing things away.

Test

M: OK, everyone, let's get started. We're going to talk about energy sources today. We're going to compare coal and wind. They're both sources of power, right? Now let's look at their similarities and then their differences.

The first question is; how long can we use these two power sources? Well, we have enough coal to last about 285 years. Wind power will last forever. Yes, Suzy?

W: So wind power is better. I mean, it will never run out. Right?

M: Yes, that's right. Good! So, one difference is that coal will run out some day. Wind power won't. That's important. However, a similarity between coal and wind is that, for now, we have plenty of each.

The methods we use to get energy affect the environment. So, let's compare the way wind and coal affect the environment. One is bad. One is good. You have to burn coal to make energy. And harmful gases are released as waste into the air when we burn coal. These gases are very bad for the environment. But all you need to make power from wind is a windmill and wind. Actually, in a way, we recycle the wind! Recycling is really just using something again. We can use wind again, and again. No waste. No pollution. No problems for the environment. So, we also see that coal and wind power have very different effects on the environment.

[Unit 9]

Conversation

Practice

M: Hi, Professor Howard. Can you help me with something?
W: Of course. What do you need?
M: Well, it's, uh, the lectures. I'm having problems. I do my best to listen and follow what you are saying. But, when the lecture is finished, I can't remember anything!
W: Hmm... I see. That's a problem. But don't worry.
M: Really?
W: Yes, you just need to work on your note-taking skills. Let me explain. (*Practice A end.*)
M: Thanks.
W: OK, the first thing you need to do is stay calm and listen carefully to the lecture. If you try to remember everything, then things will confuse you even more. Remember; just take notes on the important parts, or main ideas. Write them in your own words, too. Don't copy what I say.
M: OK.
W: Also, when the lecture is finished, go over your notes again. But don't delay. Review them right away to keep them fresh in your mind. The repetition really helps. I mean, the more you read them, the more you will remember. Also, feel free to ask me questions after class. Just don't interrupt the lecture!
M: I won't. Thanks, Professor.

Test

W: Hi, Professor Harrison. Can I talk to you?
M: Hi, Susan. What's the problem?
W: Well, it's just that I'm struggling in your lectures.
M: Oh? Am I going too fast? Am I too confusing?
W: I'm not sure how to explain it. I'm taking a lot of notes. And I review them again and again. I know repetition is important. It's just that I don't understand the lessons very well.
M: I see. Well, chemistry isn't easy.
W: Can you tell me what to do?
M: Well, first make sure to write your notes in your own words. Don't copy everything I say. And, you could join a study group. There's a group that meets twice a week at night. Other students can often offer fresh ideas about the lessons.
W: OK, I'll try that. I really want to get a good grade this semester.
M: I'm sure you'll do fine.
W: Is there anything else I should do?
M: Yes, if you are still confused you can interrupt the lecture to ask questions. Don't delay, let me know!
W: Yeah, I'll do that. Thanks for helping me!
M: No problem.

Practice

M: Today's lesson is on germs. Germs are everywhere. Many get on your hands. And if these germs get into your mouth, you can get sick. But we don't want to get sick, right? So these germs are a problem. OK, how do we solve this problem? Well, one way is to kill germs by washing your hands with soap and water. But there's a catch. Doing this might not actually kill all the germs. Let me explain... (*Practice A end.*)

OK, so we know that washing your hands can kill germs. Your parents probably remind you to wash your hands before you eat. Well, they're right. But here's the thing... you can't just do a quick rinse. You have to be very thorough. You really have to scrub your hands. When you scrub them, you remove bacteria, and other bad substances, off the first layer of your skin. So, you need to make sure you get your hands very clean. But be careful if you scrub for too long, you will hurt your hands. You should scrub your hands for about ten seconds, or about the same time it takes to sing the "Happy Birthday" song. Try it. You'll be less likely to get sick.

Test

W: Good morning! Today let's talk about antibacterial gels. Until about 15 years ago, most people used normal soap to wash their hands. Now, lots of people use antibacterial gels to remove bacteria. These gels are supposed to be better at killing germs. Anything that kills germs is a good thing, right? Wrong! Here's the problem... these gels can be bad for your hands. And they can make germs stronger and harder to kill.

Yes, antibacterial gels do kill germs. But the chemicals—the substances they use to do this—are bad for your hands. Your skin has layers that protect it. The gel removes these layers. And it leaves your hands dry and sensitive. More so, if you use these gels too often or don't rinse off the gel. Your skin will be more likely to get sores or infections.

Also, the gel can sometimes make germs stronger. Yes, Frank?

M: But if the gel kills germs, how can it make them stronger?

W: Good question. You see, the gel only kills some kinds of germs. The other germs don't die. So, they become stronger. And if you get sick from these germs, this is a problem.

Actually, most germs are killed just as well by thorough washing with soap and water. So, use normal soap more often. Just remind yourself to scrub your hands long enough to remove all the germs!

[Unit 10]

Practice

M: Excuse me. Do you work here?
W: Yes, I do. Can I help you with something?
M: Yes. I'm new here. I'm not sure how the cafeteria works.
W: OK, well there are two things you have to know. One is the cafeteria schedule. And the other is the meal plan.
M: Yeah, I haven't heard anything about either of those things.
W: Hmm... I'll tell you about them quickly.
M: That'd be great. (*Practice A end.*)
W: OK, the first thing is the schedule.
M: Yeah, I was wondering about that. Is the cafeteria open all day?
W: Well, not exactly. We are open for breakfast, lunch, and dinner. Those hours are posted on the sign on the front door.
M: Oh, that makes sense.
W: We usually have a few different choices of food. The day's menu is on the sign.

M: Do many students complain about the food?

W: [*Laughing.*] Hmm... well, everyone's taste is different! Anyway, just bring your student ID with you. You can pay cash. Or you can get a meal plan. This is where you buy credits. Each meal will take one credit off your account. This is better for most students as it is cheaper.

M: OK, sounds good. Thanks for your help!

Test

W: Hi. Do you work here?

M: Yes, I do!

W: Oh, great! I was wondering if you could tell me about the food in the cafeteria.

M: Sure! Well, you usually have two choices. You've got the food from the grill. And you've got the daily meal.

W: OK.

M: Let's start with the grill first. It's open every day.

W: What type of foods do they grill?

M: The usual. You know... hamburgers, hot dogs, chicken.

W: Oh, that sounds good. How about the daily meal?

M: That changes every day. One day might be fish, the next day might be spaghetti. It's always something new and exciting. And there is always something for everyone's taste.

W: [*Laughing.*] I'll bet!

M: So, there is one thing... you can't have both. You must choose either the grill food or the daily meal. They each use one credit from your meal plan. And the menu is always posted outside beside the cafeteria schedule.

W: Got it.

M: We also serve a lot of fruits and vegetables.

W: Great! I love vegetables.

M: Well, is there anything else I can help you with?

W: I think that's everything. I don't think I will be complaining about the food, it sounds great! Thanks so much!

Lecture

Practice

W: Hi, everyone. Today I want to talk about holograms. Do you know what those are? Well, they're three-dimensional images. Most people call them 3D images for short. And, uh, they're projected into mid-air. So how do we use them? Well, people are using them for two major things. First, advertising. And second, crime fighting! How exciting! (*Practice A end.*)

OK, so, first... advertising. Who uses 3D images for advertising? Car companies! They use them to show their newest cars. But these are not regular, small computer images. No. These images are full-size and full-color. They look just like the real thing. It's a good way to advertise. People like how they look. And it saves money, since companies don't need to build model cars. They can just press a button and show the image of the car.

These holograms are also used to fight crime. It's true! They are doing this at a university in Rome. The faculty... I mean, the teachers, make 3D images. What do they show? Well, they show signatures. You know, for things like checks. And these images are very detailed. So these people study these signatures. And they can prove if they are real or not!

Test

M: OK, let 's get started. Today's lesson is on robots. They're used in hospitals. Where? Many places all over the world. But these robots are not models that work on their own. No. Doctors control these robots. They're used in two ways. First, for viewing. And second, for doing surgery. Let's start with viewing, OK?

The ZEUS System helps doctors with surgery. It shows them three-dimensional images. It does this while they do surgery. How? Well, a tiny camera is put inside a patient. Then a doctor uses a robot to control this camera. The camera shows a projected image of the patient's body. But the doctor does not control the robot with his hands. How does he move it? By pushing a pedal... with his foot. So, this leaves his hands free to do surgery. While he is doing the surgery, he can control the camera. And it lets him view things he could never see with just his regular eyesight. So, the robot makes surgery much easier.

OK, now, the da Vinci System helps doctors to do surgery. It uses cameras... Yes, Penelope?

W: It uses cameras? Just like the other one does?

M: Yes. But, in this case, the robot actually helps to do surgery. You see, the doctor controls the robot with a joystick. And the joystick controls small surgical tools. So, the doctor makes the robot do surgery in places where his hands can't reach. Isn't that great! This proves that robots can really help doctors with surgery. And robots can save lives!

[Unit 11]

Conversation

Practice

M: Hi. I need to talk to someone about a housing problem.
W: That's me. What do you need?
M: Well, uh, it's my roommate. He listens to loud music late at night, so I want to change to a new dorm room, please.
W: Hmm... that sounds like a problem. However, I'm sorry our rules say that I can't let you change rooms just because of that. I can recommend a couple of things that might help. (*Practice A end.*)
M: OK.
W: The first thing you need to do is communicate. I mean, talk with each other. It's not always easy, but it really does help.
M: Yeah, I guess. Neither of us has really tried to solve the problem. It's just that I have a part-time job doing research for a professor, so I have to wake up early.
W: I see. Then maybe you should reach an agreement with your roommate about when he can play music.
M: Yeah. Maybe if I agree not to watch TV early in the morning, then he'll agree not to play music at night.
W: Exactly. That is a good compromise. It's give and take.
M: Hmm... I guess I can do that. I'll give it a try. Thanks.

Test

M: Hi. Do you need help?
W: Hi. My roommate and I have been thinking about painting our dorm room a new color, maybe green...
M: [*Interrupting.*] Uh, that's against our housing rules.
W: [*Should sound cheeky.*] I was hoping we could come to a compromise.
M: I'm sorry, no. If I do that for you, then all of the students will expect us to compromise with them, too.
W: I suppose you're right.
M: Have you thought about decorating your room in other ways? I mean, ways that don't break any of our housing rules?
W: [*Laughing.*] Yeah, but those ways are so boring!
M: Well, there's a couple of things I could recommend that would give your room a new look.
W: Like what?
M: For one thing, you could put pictures and posters on your walls.
W: That's true.
M: Or you could rearrange your furniture. I know, I know it's not easy. Some of that stuff is very heavy. But, it gives your room a fresh look.
W: Yeah, and it's good exercise!
M: That's right. You can decorate your room and exercise at the same time!
W: [Laughing.] Well, it's still not as fun as painting. But, what can I do? Thanks for your help.

Practice

M: OK. Let's talk about how cities grow. There is a model that explains this. It's called the Burgess model. This model splits cities up into circles. A city starts in one place, right? And then it expands into circles that get bigger and bigger. A group of circles around the center. Got it? OK. Each circle represents part of the city. Let's see, uh, the center circle is the area we call downtown. The next circle is the factory area. And the third circle is the living area. And each of these areas must develop for the city to grow. (*Practice A end.*)

The downtown area develops first. It's the heart of the city. And it's the center of the city's economy. The main transportation networks are there. What develops next? The factory area. It's next to the downtown area. This is where the industries are. Where people invest money in the city. Lots of people also work in the big factories. What's the third part to develop? It's the living area, where most of the people live, including the city workers. What happens when more people move to the city? The living area spreads farther out from the center. And that's how a city develops. It's how our city developed.

Test

W: OK, let's start. Let's talk about developing countries. There's a process they must go through, so that they can develop. OK? Let's split this process into three areas. They need to target three areas. What are these areas? First, they need to develop a good economy. Second, they need a good school system. And third, they need a strong government. OK. Have you ever heard of Moldova? It's a small country in Europe. Let's use it as a model to examine what we're going to talk about.

All right... so Moldova has a stable economy. It's been expanding for the past seven years. Why? Well, farming is their main source of money. So what did the government do? It sold the farmland to the people who live in Moldova. Now they make more money. Yes, Ron?

M: More money is good for their economy, right?

W: Exactly.

OK. Developing countries also need good schools. And you know what? Moldova has special types of schools. They're called community schools. These schools help teach kids about jobs. Not just any jobs. Community jobs that will be needed. Jobs that'll be there when the kids grow up. Smart, huh?

The third thing a developing country needs is a strong government. OK, this is where Moldova has problems. Why? The government has not worked well with other countries. They need to get other countries to invest money in their country. The government needs to do better here. This is important. Why? Because they need money to develop. Got it?

[Unit 12]

Practice

M: Ms. Garcia, could I please talk with you?
W: Sure, Jacob. What do you need?
M: I'm upset. I failed the geometry test. I got so many questions wrong. I think I need some extra help.
W: Don't worry, Jacob. I know of a couple things you could do. First, let's talk about making some extra time to review before the tests. And second, you may be interested in a tutoring program I know about. (*Practice A end.*)
M: OK. Sounds good.
W: Please remember you're a great student. But geometry can be tricky at times. Don't get discouraged. If you'd like to stay after school the day before the tests, we can take time to do extra practice just for you. Sometimes just going over the formulas a few more times helps.

M: Thanks, Ms. Garcia. I think that would help me a lot.

W: Now, let me tell you about this new tutoring program.

M: Uh... I don't think my parents can afford tutoring.

W: No Jacob, this tutoring is free. It's at the library on the corner. There are volunteers there who help students with schoolwork. They're good. They won't confuse you.

M: That sounds good too. I'm glad I talked to you, Ms. Garcia.

Test

W: Excuse me, Mr. Dawson. Do you have a minute?

M: Hi, Rachel. What can I do for you?

W: Oh! I see you're getting ready to leave.

M: That's OK. What did you need?

W: I didn't do very well on my geometry test. Would you have time—maybe tomorrow—to go over the test with me? I got so many questions wrong.

M: Sure, Rachel. What time?

W: I could come in early before your first class.

M: That would be great. Let's say seven-thirty. First, tell me what's giving you the most trouble?

W: I've always been so good at mathematics. I used to be a volunteer math tutor at my old school and I have even given math lessons! Geometry, though, is really tricky. I don't understand the formulas.

M: Do the reviews in the textbook help?

W: Yes, but I just can't seem to remember everything when I'm taking the tests.

M: I think a little extra practice is all you need. You'll be fine.

W: I hope so. I am getting really discouraged and I don't want to get another bad test grade.

M: Don't worry. We'll go over all the questions you missed tomorrow morning.

Lecture

Practice

W: You know what. Sometimes, changing one thing has an effect on many things. Like recording equipment. It changed music. We can listen to music anywhere. But that's not my point. My point is that it changed the way music sounds! Let's look at how one style of music changed. It's called vibrato. Do you recognize that word? No? OK. (*Practice A end.*)

OK, this style of music is when the sound, the, uh, the tone of a musical note goes up and down very fast. It's almost, a shaking sound. Violins make this sound often. Well, people didn't start using this sort of sound until they could record music. Why is that? Because they used only one microphone to record music. This made it hard to hear all the different sounds. Especially the string instruments. Strings aren't as loud as drums, right? So louder instruments would interfere with the sound of the strings. And this was a big problem. So how did they fix this? They started using vibrato during recording sessions. Why? Because it helped people hear the separate sounds of the different instruments. And then people could notice the sound of the strings. See? That's how recording equipment changed that style of music. Got it?

Test

M: Good morning. Today, I'm going to tell you about a famous jazz musician. His name was Duke Ellington. In the 1920s, jazz wasn't as popular as it is now. People didn't really notice jazz. But he made it very popular. How? Well, his music was heard all over America. And he liked to write and record his own songs. So, he helped make jazz popular.

Duke Ellington got his music heard all over America. And I'm not just talking about concerts. Many musicians played in concerts. They had good equipment, like microphones, for live music sessions. And they went to many places. But Duke Ellington was different. How? You see, his music was on national radio. Back then, it was a big deal to get on the radio. It really was. And Ellington was one of the first to have jazz played on the radio. Lots of people could listen to it. It was national radio, you see. Almost everyone could hear it. And you know what? People really liked it.

OK, he did something else that helped him to succeed. What did he do? He wrote his own music. And recorded it. This was a big deal. Why? Because he became known as a composer... you know... someone who writes music. And he was very good. His music was original. Before Duke, people didn't notice jazz much. And they didn't recognize it as a separate form of music. But after Duke, they sure did. So really, he was the one who made jazz popular.

[Review 2]

Conversation 1

W: Hi, Professor. Do you have a second?

M: Yes! What do you need?

W: It's about our group project. We failed. We spent a lot of time on it, and we're a little discouraged.

M: I did like your theme. But you failed to develop it fully. If you had expanded upon your ideas, you would have passed.

W: One of our group members didn't help. He kept interrupting the other members. He interfered with our progress.

M: You think that you failed because of him?

W: Yes. Additionally, he isn't majoring in this program, so I don't think he wanted to try very hard. I don't like to criticize anyone, but he's the reason we couldn't get the work done on time.

M: Well, if your group had communicated this to me a few weeks ago, we could have done something about it. But, it's too late now.

W: But it wasn't our fault!

M: I shouldn't have to remind you that when you get out into the real world you won't always get to choose who you work with. This project was supposed to prepare you for that experience. Anyway, there is a review coming up soon. You'll have a chance to get better grades then.

W: [*Dejectedly.*] OK. Thanks.

Lecture 1

M: OK, class. So, most people recognize that the environment is in danger. There have been many changes compared to twenty years ago, but there is still a long way to go. Many people have seen the layers of smog above our city. This is an example of how we affect our world. We have to take action to save our environment. There are three ways we can help.

First, people can do things themselves. We can reduce the amount of garbage that we produce. One way to do this is to recycle. This is a good first step. It will get rid of extra waste. You could plan recycling programs in your local area. Students could go door to door to collect recyclable goods. They could take them to a community recycling center. Stores could even offer credit to people who bring back recyclable goods.

Then, we need to elect strong leaders. We need a person that has a good plan for clean air. We need a person who will demand cleaner cars.

Finally, we need these leaders to look for new methods to get rid of harmful substances. They could build special equipment. Perhaps equipment that will make fuel that is not harmful for the environment. Or that will make recycling easier.

A clean environment it is good for the planet. It's good for the economy. And it's good for us. It's up to you to prove that we are serious about a clean planet.

Lecture 2

W: These days the public is worried about bird flu. This new flu is not just for birds. It could make many people sick or even die. You should not confuse regular flu with bird flu. While the normal flu can make you very sick, the bird flu is much stronger. Sixty percent of people who catch bird flu die.

The first sign of bird flu will be its symptoms. They are similar to regular flu such as fever, cough, sore throat, and muscle aches. There may also be eye infections and pneumonia. If you think you have the flu, your next step should be to see your doctor without delay.

For a small fee, your doctor will perform a thorough examination. If you have the flu, the doctor will want to find out which kind of flu you have. A special test is needed to find bird flu in humans. If the doctor finds that you have bird flu he will treat you.

The treatment for bird flu is not much different from regular flu. Drugs used for regular flu should work with bird flu. However, the flu might change. If it does, these drugs might not work. Your doctor may want to send you to the hospital. You should also rest and drink lots of water.

Faculties at top schools are working on a formula that could stop bird flu. They are practicing ways to stop it. This may take many years and much repetition before we see any results. It will take time, but the effort will be worth it.

Lecture 3

M: Good morning! Are we ready? OK. Oils spills. One of the worst disasters we can face is an oil spill. In 1989, a large ship sank off Alaska. Over forty million liters of oil escaped into the sea. This killed many animals and hurt the local economy. Then the U.S. President was unhappy because the clean up was not very quick or easy. This was because the machines to do it were not good.

Today, new machines make it easier to clean up oil spills. One example is the new grooved oil skimmer. It was invented at the University of California. This invention will allow faster and easier cleanup of oil spills.

The skimmer is a large drum that spins over the surface of an oil spill. The oil tends to stick to the drum. Then the machine separates the oil from the drum. The oil is put it into a special container where it is reserved for later use. The new skimmer shares many similarities with the old style skimmer. The main difference is that the spinning drum can pick up even more oil. This makes it quicker and easier to use.

Other good news is that some countries have agreed to lend their oil skimmers to other countries. This new invention has made a big difference to how we deal with oil spills. But helping each other remains the best way to keep our oceans clean and safe.

Conversation 2

M: Hi! I was wondering if you could help me.
W: What's the problem?
M: I'd like to change dorm rooms. I can't live with my roommate any longer.
W: Can you give me some more details?
M: Well, I don't like to complain, but we're just too different. He never cleans up after himself. And we have different schedules. He comes home late every night and wakes me up.
W: Has he broken any of the dorm's rules that you know of?
M: Well, there are dirty dishes from the cafeteria all over the floor. But, I don't want him to get into trouble. He's actually a good guy. I like him, but I just can't live with him.
W: OK. Have you tried to talk to him? Maybe you could work out some sort of compromise.
M: I've tried that. He promises that he'll be more considerate, but nothing changes. I'd move out on my own, but I can't afford to. Also, I need to improve my grades this session and I need to study in a cleaner, quieter place.
W: Okay, if it's that bad, I'll talk to the dorm manager and recommend that we find a new room for you.
M: Thanks a lot.

Answer Key

[Unit 1]

Page 18-19

A

1. B   2. A

B

Woman - Student	Man - University Employee
• Wants an ID <u>for the computer lab</u> • First semester - needs one for <u>science class</u>	• Most freshman classes need an <u>ID and password</u> • Passwords are <u>important</u> • Want privacy then you have to have <u>passwords</u> • People can steal <u>personal information</u> • Tells woman to fill out form with <u>name, address, and password</u> • Should be able to use <u>tomorrow</u>

C

1. A   2. B   3. A

D

1. Freshmen   2. semesters   3. ID
4. professor   5. privacy

Page 20

Man - Student	Woman - University Employee
• Never sent an <u>email</u> • Already has ID and password and is <u>logged on</u> • Already knows <u>and thinks it's interesting</u>	• Thinks he will learn <u>pretty fast</u> • Put arrow over picture to <u>take to email</u> • Professor will <u>explain</u> • <u>Type the email address and message</u> • <u>Shouldn't send personal information because of privacy</u> • <u>Click on send</u>

1. B   2. A   3. B
4. False, True, True, True

Page 22-23

A

1. B   2. A   3. B   4. A

B and C

Underlined answers are from part B.

D

1. A   2. B   3. A

E

1. compete   2. suspicions   3. military
4. political   5. nuclear

Page 24-25

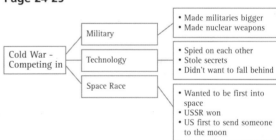

1. D   2. A   3. B   4. C
5. D   6. False, True, True, True, True

Page 26

A

1. C   2. D

B

1. weapons   2. password   3. logging into
4. personal information   5. aggressive
6. opinion

Answer Key

[Unit 2]

A

1. A   2. B

B

Man - Student	Woman - University Employee
• Needs books <u>for chemistry class</u>	• Professor Jenkins has <u>revised the lists</u>
	• Asks if he has <u>the updated list</u>
	• Professor has replaced <u>some books</u>
	• He needs <u>the course number</u>
• The office is <u>across campus</u>	• He can find the number at <u>the Professor's office</u>
• Knows computer lab is <u>open and decides to go there</u>	• Tells him he can <u>get it online</u>
	• The computer lab is <u>close</u>

C

1. A   2. B   3. A

D

1. Email   2. chemistry   3. updated
4. campus   5. revise

Page 30

Woman - Student	Man - University Employee
• Saw bookstore's <u>online update</u>	
• Goes to get <u>chemistry book</u>	• Store has just got them
• Wants a <u>used version</u>	• Asks if she can <u>wait</u>
• <u>Is low on money</u>	• Used books are <u>cheaper</u>
	• <u>Already written on</u>
	• <u>She won't be able to start studying immediately</u>
• <u>Decides to revise what she spends money on</u>	• <u>The bookstore and computer lab needs workers</u>
• <u>Thinks about working</u>	

1. A   2. A   3. D   4. A

A

1. A   2. A   3. B   4. A

B and C

Underlined answers are from part B.

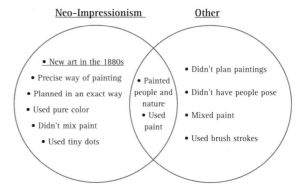

D

1. A   2. B   3. B

E

1. Various   2. purpose   3. precise
4. represent   5. reproduce

Page 34-35

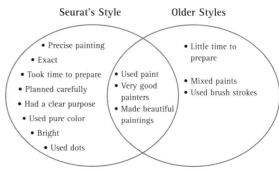

1. D   2. C   3. D   4. B
5. D   6. True, False, True, True

Page 36

A

1. A　　　　　2. C

B

1. computer lab
2. plan　　　3. exact　　　4. courses
5. online　　6. scenes

[Unit 3]

Conversation

Page 38-39

A

1. B　　　　　2. A

B

Man - Student	Woman - Professor
• Asks how to write a <u>good essay</u> • Takes many notes and <u>understands the lessons but essays not good</u>	• Tells the student that a good essay needs <u>organization</u> • Goes over the <u>format</u> • Three <u>parts to an essay</u> 　1. <u>Introduction</u> 　　- gives the main idea 　2. Body <u>paragraphs</u> 　　- provides <u>evidence or details</u> 　3. Conclusion 　　- is <u>a summary</u> • Tells the student that good <u>organization is important</u>

C

1. A　　　　2. A　　　　3. B

D

1. format　　2. paragraph　3. summary
4. evidence　5. organization

Page 40

Woman - Student	Man - Professor
• Needs help with <u>essay</u> • Is having problems <u>finding good information</u> • Not good <u>at taking notes</u> • <u>Was reading a lot and copies down too much</u>	• Talks about finding <u>good information first</u> • Books are <u>best</u> • Can look <u>online too</u> • <u>Internet—type in subject get list</u> • <u>Books—search on library computer</u> • <u>Take notes</u> • <u>Summary, read introduction and conclusion first</u> • <u>Take notes that give evidence</u> • <u>Organization of notes is important</u>

1. D　　　　2. B　　　　3. D　　　　4. C

Lecture

Page 42-43

A

1. B　　　　2. B　　　　3. B　　　　4. A

B and C

Underlined answers are from part B.

Bats in Winter

Problem	Solution
• <u>Is cold</u> • <u>Hard to find food</u>	• <u>Hibernate</u> to stay warm and survive the winter
• Sensitive to cold • Can't live through winter	• Sleep together in caves • Shield from the cold
• Hard to find food	• Eat more in fall • Live off body fat

D

1. A　　　　2. B　　　　3. A

E

1. creature　　2. shield
3. average　　4. sensitive　　5. solving

Page 44-45

Snakes

Problem	Solution
Getting Eaten →	→ Unique ways of protecting themselves
• Rattlesnake →	• Small beads on tail • Beads rub and make rattling sound • Cannot shield itself so scares
• Spitting cobra →	• Sprays poison from its mouth into eyes • Stops creature from seeing • Snake gets away
• Hognose snake →	• Plays dead • Twists and rolls then lies still and hangs tongue out of its mouth

1. B   2. C   3. D   4. A
5. A   6. True, True, False, True, False

Check-up

Page 46
A
1. C   2. A

B
1. deep sleep 2. introduction 3. underground
4. essay   5. lessons   6. disappear

[Unit 4]

Conversation

Page 48-49
A
1. B   2. A

B

Woman - Student	Man - Librarian

• Needs help to <u>check out library books</u>
• Has to do <u>research for an essay</u>
 	
• Has a student library <u>account</u>
	• Two choices:
	  1. use the <u>self-service machine</u>
	  2. go to <u>the front desk</u>
	• Self-service machine:
	  - looks like <u>a computer</u>
	  - scan <u>ID</u>
	  - then <u>scan book</u>
	  - machine will print <u>receipt</u>
	  - press ID and books because <u>it is sensitive</u>
	• Take books to <u>front desk</u>
	  - librarian will <u>help</u>

C
1. A   2. B   3. A

D
1. due   2. receipt   3. research
4. scan   5. account

Page 50

Man - Student	Woman - Librarian

• Is doing research for <u>a history essay and is trying to find a book</u>
• Doesn't know where <u>to begin</u>
• Asks how the book lists work
 	
• This he can find what he needs
	• There are two ways:
	  1. computer <u>system</u>
	  2. book <u>lists</u>
	• Book lists:
	  - organize by <u>subject</u>
	  - look under <u>"History"</u>
	  - <u>then at title</u>
	  - <u>is alphabetical</u>
	  - <u>numbers tell where to find</u>
	• Computer is easy:
	  - <u>do a search</u>
	  - <u>will tell you where</u>
	• Check-out:
	  - <u>scan ID at self-service machine</u>
	  - <u>if books are due can't check out more</u>

1. C   2. C   3. C   4. A

Lecture

Page 52-53
A
1. A   2. B   3. A   4. C

B and C
Underlined answers are from part B.

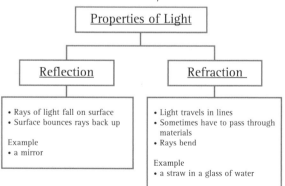

Properties of Light

Reflection	Refraction
• Rays of light fall on surface • Surface bounces rays back up Example • a mirror	• Light travels in lines • Sometimes have to pass through materials • Rays bend Example • a straw in a glass of water

D

1. A   2. A   3. A

E

1. lecture   2. repeat   3. remember
4. property   5. materials

Page 54-55

```
                    Heat Transfer
        ┌────────────────┼────────────────┐
    Convection       Conduction        Radiation
```

Convection	Conduction	Radiation

• Heat moves through gases and liquids
• When air or water heat up they get lighter —they rise
• Get cooler and come down
• Repeats
• Example—a hot air balloon
	• Heat moves through solids
	• Solid object on heat
	• Takes heat
	• Some materials very good
	• Example—metals
	  - cooking pans
		• Can feel heat without touching
		• Can't see
		• Examples:
		  - sun
		  - toaster
		  - dryer
		  - fire

1. B   2. C   3. D   4. D
5. B   6. True, True, False, True, True

Check-up

Page 56

A

1. B   2. D

B

1. self-service   2. pressed   3. check out
4. directions   5. bounce   6. ray

[Unit 5]

Conversation

Page 58-59

A

1. B   2. A

B

Man - Student	Woman - Tutor
• Asks if the woman is <u>in charge</u> • Needs help with <u>math work</u> • Doesn't want either <u>to get punished</u> • Thinks <u>it is fair</u>	• Tells the man she <u>tutors there</u> • Is a <u>math major</u> • Can help but <u>needs to clarify rules</u> • Some things she can <u>help with, some things she can't</u> • Rules against <u>cheating</u> • If cheat then <u>get kicked out of school</u> • Can help with learning strategies, <u>studying, taking notes</u> • With class work and <u>homework on his own</u>

C

1. B   2. B   3. A

D

1. strategies   2. major   3. clarify
4. tutor   5. standard

Page 60

Woman - Student	Man - Tutor
• Having problems in <u>math class</u> • Doesn't understand professor's <u>comments</u> • <u>Hasn't been going to the lectures because she is not a math major</u> • <u>Needs to prepare more</u>	 • Decides on some <u>strategies</u> • <u>Usually one or two things that can be fixed</u> • <u>Asks if she has been going to the lectures</u> • <u>Going to the lectures will help with understanding</u> • <u>Extra math exercises would help understand basic lessons</u> • <u>Thinks she is cheating herself</u>

1. C   2. D   3. B   4. D

Answer Key

A

1. B 　　　 2. A 　　　 3. B 　　　 4. C

B and C

Underlined answers are from part B.

Billboard Advertising

Know the product	Choose the focus	Choose the picture
• What does it do? • Why buy it? • Who buys it? Example - Milk	• What you want the ad to do • Usually get the customer to buy Example - get more people to drink more	• Has to look good • Has to support the ad's focus Example - shows a famous person drinking milk

D

1. B 　　　 2. A 　　　 3. B

E

1. attract` 　　　 2. focus 　　　 3. Promoting
4. process 　　　 5. attention

Page 64-65

The Four P's

Product	Price	Place	Promotion
• Make a product to sell Example • Computer Games • Study games and potential customers	• Decide on a price Example • What others charge for games • What people will spend	• Find a place to sell • Somewhere customers go Example • Online • Computer stores	• Usually advertising • Get customers to buy • Attract attention Example • TV • Billboards • Magazines • Online

1. B 　　　 2. C 　　　 3. A 　　　 4. B
5. B 　　　 6. A

Check-up

Page 66

A

1. C 　　　 2. A

B

1. cheats 　　　 2. mathematics
3. punished 　　　 4. couple
5. support 　　　 6. billboard

[Unit 6]

Conversation

Page 68-69

A

1. A 　　　 2. B

B

Woman - Student	Man - Professor
• Wants an <u>extension</u> • Has been <u>sick and was absent</u> • Needs a good grade or <u>could lose scholarship</u>	• Can't <u>give extension</u> • Can suggest <u>ways to make up</u> • Tells her to borrow <u>a classmate's notes</u> • Or go to the library and <u>do the research</u> • He can give <u>an outline of the lectures</u> • She can look up <u>the main information</u> • Thinks she will be <u>fine</u>

C

1. A 　　　 2. B 　　　 3. False, True, False

D

1. tuition 　　　 2. scholarship
3. projects 　　　 4. extension 　　　 5. grades

Page 70

Man - Student	Woman - Professor
• Has a problem with <u>a classmate</u> • Isn't doing work and <u>is absent most of the time</u> • Is going to need <u>an extension</u> • <u>Has done all his work and given him an outline</u> • <u>Grades are important</u> • <u>Needs scholarship or can't pay tuition</u> • <u>Wants to change partners</u>	 • She <u>can help</u> • Is happy with <u>student's tutoring</u> • <u>Two choices - tell partner to work harder or give new partner</u> • <u>Will tell who new partner is in a day</u>

1. D 　　　 2. B 　　　 3. A
4. Student, Professor, Professor, Professor

Lecture

Page 72-73

A

1. A   2. A   3. B   4. C

B and C

Underlined answers are from part B.

Cosmic Rays

Cause		Effect
• Cosmic rays	→	• Earth's <u>temperature</u>
• Energy from the sun	→	• Make clouds
• Rays hit Earth	→	• Break into tiny electrical particles
• Particles	→	• Attract water
• Water gathers	→	• Clouds are formed
• Clouds	→	• Bounce heat back into space
• More clouds	→	• Earth is cooler
• Fewer cosmic rays	→	• Fewer clouds
• Fewer clouds	→	• Higher temperatures

D

1. B   2. A   3. A

E

1. temperature   2. proof   3. affected
4. particles   5. cause

Page 74-75

Cause		Effect
• Small particles of metal, screws, and paint	→	• Become dangerous space junk that floats in space
• Junk such as paint moves fast	→	• Made a dent on a shuttle a couple inches deep
• Stronger material used on the outside of shuttles	→	• Space junk will cause less damage
• Shuttles fly backwards	→	• Protects the most important equipment on the front

1. B   2. B   3. A   4. D
5. B   6. C

Check-up

Page 76

A

1. D   2. C

B

1. classmates   2. absent   3. outline
4. Cosmic   5. Earth   6. space

[Review 1]

Conversation 1

Page 77

Man - Student	Woman - Professor
• He is in the professor's <u>chemistry class</u> • Has missed a lot of classes because <u>of a cold</u> • <u>Has missed every class for two weeks</u> • <u>Knows a girl who lives near</u>	• Asks for doctors note • Is glad he <u>came</u> • Gives students <u>a handout that contains a summary</u> • <u>She can give him those</u> • <u>He should also get lecture notes from a classmate</u> • <u>Can clarify anything confusing</u>

1. C   2. D   3. A   4. C

Lecture 1

Page 78-79

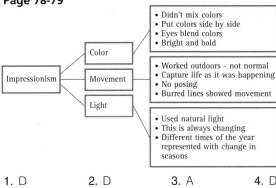

1. D   2. D   3. A   4. D
5. B   6. True, False, False, True, False

Lecture 2

Page 80-81

Bears   Pandas

- Are dangerous
- Are hunters
- Live alone
- Hibernate

- Have fur, four legs, small ears, and long nose
- Are dangerous when protecting babies
- Are hunted

- Usually peaceful
- Eat plants
- Not usually dangerous
- Live in small groups
- Do not hibernate
- Going extinct
- Losing homes

Answer Key

1. C   2. B   3. B
4. B   5. C
6. Both, Other Bears, Pandas, Other Bears, Pandas

Lecture 3
Page 82-83

Problem	Solution
• Everything stopped when the sun went down	→ • Electricity - now can do business all night
• Using oil to heat homes was not clean	→ • Nuclear Power - doesn't pollute the air but is dangerous
• Took a long time to heat food	→ • Microwave Ovens - heat food quickly
• Difficult to send TV pictures from far away	→ • Microwaves - more practical and can watch TV pictures faster

1. D   2. D   3. B   4. A
5. D   6. Yes, Yes, Yes, No, No

Conversation 2
Page 84

Woman - Student	Man - University Employee
• Wants to borrow a book • Her professor said it would help her research	• Tells student it is a reference book so can't borrow it • Tells student she can do research there as she can't take reference books home • There is a lot of demand for reference material
• Asks how to find journal articles	• Do a search on library database • It will give a list of articles • Write them down and take them to the reference section
• Asks about regular books • Asks when they are due	• Show proof you are a student • He will scan and she can take them home • Most books due back in three weeks

1. B   2. C   3. D
4. reference material, novel, novel, reference material

[Unit 7]

Conversation
Page 86-87

A
1. B   2. A

B

Woman - Student	Man - University Employee
• Wants to use the Sports Center	• Needs to do two things: open an account and pay for a locker • Show student ID and he will print a membership card • Is open to the public but students don't pay • People tend to get a locker at each visit • Can pay to use one that is only hers • Will lend a towel each time
• Decides to pay for a locker	• If she wants to use a court then she has to reserve

C
1. A   2. B   3. B

D
1. Public   2. tend   3. lend
4. fees   5. reserved

Page 88

Man - Student	Woman - University Employee
• Would like to reserve a tennis court • Has a gym membership	• Two ways • Can reserve in person at the front desk • They are open to the public • Mornings and evenings tend to be busiest • Can also call before coming • Employee will take name and time • Fee is included in the membership • Will lend a tennis racket and balls • Lockers are down the hall

1. A   2. C   3. D   4. A

Lecture

Page 90-91

A

1. A   2. A   3. B   4. A

B and C

Underlined answers are from part B.

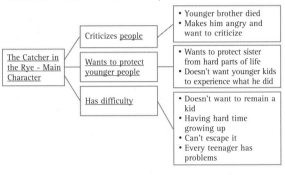

The Catcher in the Rye - Main Character	Criticizes people	• Younger brother died • Makes him angry and want to criticize
	Wants to protect younger people	• Wants to protect sister from hard parts of life • Doesn't want younger kids to experience what he did
	Has difficulty	• Doesn't want to remain a kid • Having hard time growing up • Can't escape it • Every teenager has problems

D

1. A   2. B   3. A

E

1. criticize   2. experiences
3. escape   4. theme   5. remaining

Page 92-93

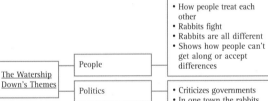

The Watership Down's Themes	People	• How people treat each other • Rabbits fight • Rabbits are all different • Shows how people can't get along or accept differences
	Politics	• Criticizes governments • In one town the rabbits have no freedom • In the other town things are too easy • Shows how no government is perfect

1. C   2. B   3. A   4. A
5. A   6. True, True, True, False

Check-up

Page 94

A

1. A   2. B

B

1. locker   2. adult   3. courts
4. membership 5. teenager   6. grow up

[Unit 8]

Conversation

Page 96-97

A

1. B   2. A

B

Woman - Student	Man - Activities Director
• Just moved would like to join a club • Was president of old school's chess club • Would like to do something different • Would like to help	• Have two types of clubs: sports and games and community service. • Need to choose a club then get a membership • Chess club is going to officers soon • Community service clubs tutor kids or help elderly people • Thinks it's important for young people to help

C

1. A   2. B   3. B

D

1. president   2. elected   3. local
4. community   5. additional

Page 98

Man - Student	Woman - Professor
• Asks if she helps the chess club • Asks who they elected as president • Is interested in joining a club • Thinks a sports club would be good • Asks for a list • Will go after class or check online	• Was close but Justin was elected • Lists on the school website or the sports office next to the health center • Helps with community service club

1. B   2. D   3. C   4. A

Answer Key

Lecture

Page 100-101

A

1. A   2. B   3. A   4. B

B and C

Underlined answers are from part B.

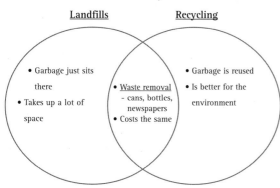

Landfills   Recycling

- Garbage just sits there
- Takes up a lot of space

- <u>Waste removal - cans, bottles, newspapers</u>
- Costs the same

- Garbage is reused
- Is better for the environment

D

1. A   2. B   3. A

E

1. environment   2. methods   3. recycled
4. similarities   5. compares

Page 102-103

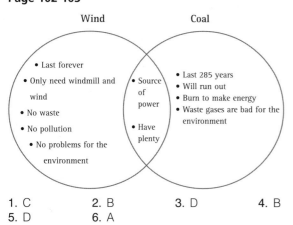

Wind   Coal

- Last forever
- Only need windmill and wind
- No waste
- No pollution
- No problems for the environment

- Source of power
- Have plenty

- Last 285 years
- Will run out
- Burn to make energy
- Waste gases are bad for the environment

1. C   2. B   3. D   4. B
5. D   6. A

Check-up

Page 104

A

1. B   2. A

B

1. Chess   2. waste   3. landfills
4. elderly   5. service   6. space

[Unit 9]

Conversation

Page 106-107

A

1. B   2. A

B

Man - Student	Woman - Professor
• Needs <u>help</u> • Is having <u>problems in the lectures</u> • Does best to <u>listen and follow</u> • When the lecture <u>is finished can't remember anything</u>	• Tells the student <u>not to worry</u> • Work on <u>note-taking skills</u> • Stay calm and <u>listen</u> • Take notes on <u>the important parts or main ideas</u> • Write them in own <u>words</u> • When the lecture is finished, <u>review notes</u> • Repetition <u>helps</u> • Can ask questions but <u>don't interrupt the lecture</u>

C

1. B   2. A   3. A

D

1. confuse   2. review   3. interrupt
4. repetition   5. delayed

Page 108

Woman - Student	Man - Professor
• Is struggling in <u>lecture</u> • Is taking a lot of <u>notes and is reviewing them</u> • Doesn't understand <u>the lessons</u> • <u>Wants a good grade</u>	• Asks if he is too <u>fast or confusing</u> • Thinks chemistry <u>isn't easy</u> • Write notes in <u>own words</u> • <u>Join a study group</u> • <u>A group meets twice a week</u> • <u>Can interrupt the lecture to ask questions</u>

1. B   2. B   3. D   4. D

Lecture

Page 110-111

A

1. A   2. A   3. B   4. C

B and C

Underlined answers are from part B.

Killing Germs

Problem	Solution
• <u>Germs on hands</u> • <u>Germs get into mouth</u>	→ • <u>Wash hands with soap and water</u>
• Not all germs killed • Can't just rinse	→ • Be thorough • Scrub hands to remove bacteria off the first layer
• Scrubbing for too long will hurt hands	→ • Scrub for about 10 seconds • Or for same time as it takes to sing "Happy Birthday"

D
1. A   2. B   3. A

E
1. reminded   2. layers   3. substance
4. thorough   5. remove

Page 112-113

Antibacterial Gels

Problem	Solution

• Bad for hands
  - gel removes layers on hands
  - leaves hands dry and sensitive
	→ • Don't use too often
	
	• Rinse off gel

• Makes germs stronger
  - makes germs harder to kill
  - only kills some germs
	→ • Use normal soap more often

1. B   2. C   3. B   4. D
5. C   6. A

Check-up
Page 114

A
1. D   2. A

B
1. scrub   2. Rinsing   3. bacteria
4. fresh   5. copy   6. calm

[Unit 10]

Conversation Practice
Page 116-117

A
1. A   2. A

B

Man - Student	Woman - Cafeteria Employee
• Is new and is not <u>sure how the cafeteria works</u> • Asks if many students <u>complain</u>	• Tell the student he needs to know two things: <u>the cafeteria schedule and the meal plan</u> • It is open for <u>breakfast, lunch, and dinner</u> • Hours are posted on <u>the sign on the front door</u> • Menu is on <u>the sign</u> • Laughs and says everyone's <u>taste is different</u> • Should bring <u>student ID</u> • Can pay cash or <u>get a meal plan</u> • Each meal takes <u>one credit off his account</u> • This is <u>cheaper</u>

C
1. A   2. B   3. A

D
1. schedule   2. complain   3. credit
4. wonder   5. cafeteria

Page 118

Woman - Student	Man - Cafeteria Employee
• Wants to know about <u>the food in the cafeteria</u> • <u>Loves vegetables</u> • <u>Won't be complaining, it sounds great</u>	• Have two choices: <u>food from the grill and the daily meal</u> • The grill is open <u>everyday</u> • Hamburgers, <u>hot dogs, chicken</u> • The daily meal changes <u>everyday</u> • <u>Something for everyone's taste</u> • <u>Must choose either grill or daily meal</u> • <u>They each use one credit</u> • <u>Menu is posted outside beside the schedule</u> • <u>Also serve a lot of fruit and vegetables</u>

1. B   2. D   3. B   4. D

Lecture

Page 120-121

A

1. B 2. A 3. A 4. C

B and C

Underlined answers are from part B.

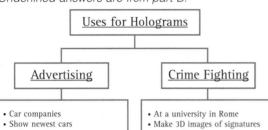

Uses for Holograms

Advertising	Crime Fighting
• Car companies • Show newest cars • Full-size, full-color • Look real • Saves money • Don't need to build model cars	• At a university in Rome • Make 3D images of signatures • For checks • Images are very detailed • Can study signatures and prove if they are real

D

1. A 2. A 3. B

E

1. images 2. regular 3. faculty
4. project 5. prove

Page 122-123

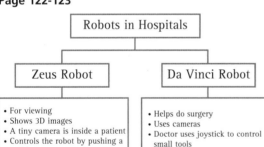

Robots in Hospitals

Zeus Robot	Da Vinci Robot
• For viewing • Shows 3D images • A tiny camera is inside a patient • Controls the robot by pushing a pedal • Lets him see things he could never see with just regular eyes • Makes surgery easier	• Helps do surgery • Uses cameras • Doctor uses joystick to control small tools • Robot does surgery in places the doctor can't reach

1. D 2. A 3. A 4. C
5. B 6. B

Check-up

Page 124

A

1. D 2. A

B

1. menu 2. post 3. model
4. taste 5. three-dimensional
6. signature

[Unit 11]

Conversation

Page 126-127

A

1. B 2. A

B

Man - Student	Woman - University Employee
• Needs to talk to <u>someone about a housing problem</u> • His roommate <u>listens to loud music late at night</u> • Wants to <u>change rooms</u>	• Can't let him <u>change rooms</u> • Can recommend <u>a couple of things</u> • Communicate; it is not <u>always easy but helps</u>
• Neither have tried to <u>solve the problem</u> • Has a part-time job doing <u>research and has to wake up early</u> • Thinks he could not <u>watch TV in the morning</u>	• Should reach an agreement about <u>when he can play music</u> • Thinks <u>it's a good compromise</u>

C

1. A 2. B 3. A

D

1. compromise 2. communicate
3. dorm 4. recommend 5. rules

Page 128

Woman - Student	Man - University Employee
• Roommate and her thinking about <u>painting dorm room green</u> • Was hoping for <u>a</u>	• Painting is against <u>housing rules</u>
• <u>Thinks they are boring</u> • <u>Thinks it's not as fun as painting</u>	• Can't compromise • Could decorate in ways that don't break rules • Put pictures and posters on walls • <u>Rearrange furniture</u>

1. C 2. D 3. B 4. A

Lecture

Page 130-131

A

1. A 2. A 3. B 4. C

B and C

Underlined answers are from part B.

City Development – Burgess Model

Downtown		Factory Area		Living Area
• Heart of the city • Center of city's economy • Main transportation network	→	• Where industries are • Where people invest money • People work in big factories	→	• Where people live • Spreads out

D
1. B   2. A   3. A

E
1. economy   2. expands   3. develop
4. area   5. invest

Page 132-133

Developing Country – Moldova

Economy		Schools		Government
• Stable • Has been expanding for 7 years • Farming is main source of money • Government sold farmland to the people	→	• Has community schools • Teach kids about jobs • Jobs that will be needed when the kids grow up	→	• Has problems • Government has not worked well with other countries • They need to get other countries to invest • Need more money to develop

1. A   2. B   3. A   4. B
5. D`   6. D

Check-up

Page 134

A
1. C   2. D

B
1. split   2. transportation
3. part-time   4. roommates
5. job   6. model

[Unit 12]

Conversation

Page 136-137

A
1. A   2. B

B

Man - Student	Woman - Professor
• Is <u>upset</u> • Failed the <u>geometry test</u>	• Knows a couple of things he can do: <u>making time to review and a tutoring program</u> • Geometry can be <u>tricky</u> • Don't get <u>discouraged</u> • Can stay after <u>school and do extra practice</u>
• Thinks that <u>would help</u> • Can't <u>afford tutoring</u>	• Going over the <u>formulas helps</u> • New tutoring program Is <u>free at the library on the corner</u> • Volunteers help <u>students with work and are good and won't confuse</u>

C
1. A   2. A   3. True, False, False

D
1. formula   2. discouraged
3. program   4. practice   5. afford

Conversation Test

Page 138

Woman - Student	Man - Professor
• Didn't do well on <u>geometry test</u> • Always been good at <u>math</u> • Used to be a <u>volunteer math tutor at school</u> • <u>Doesn't understand the formulas</u> • <u>Can't remember everything when taking the test</u> • <u>Is getting discouraged</u> • <u>Doesn't want another bad grade</u>	• Can meet at 7:30 • Asks if the reviews <u>help</u> • <u>Thinks she needs extra practice and will be fine</u> • <u>Will go over questions tomorrow</u>

1. A   2. C   3. B   4. C

Lecture

Page 140-141

A
1. A   2. A   3. B   4. B

Answer Key

B and C

Underlined answers are from part B.

Cause		Effect
• <u>Recording equipment made</u>	→	• Changed how music sounds
• Only one microphone was used	→	• Used vibrato so people could hear the different instruments

D
1. A   2. A   3. A

E
1. interfere   2. separate   3. recognized
4. equipment   5. session

Page 142-143

Cause		Effect
• Ellington got jazz played on the national radio • Was one of the first jazz musicians to do so	→	• Everyone across the country got to hear jazz • Lots of people started to like it
• Wrote and recorded his own music	→	• Became known as a composer • Made Jazz popular

1. A   2. B   3. C   4. A
5. D   6. B

Check-up

Page 144

A
1. C   2. D

B
1. microphone   2. geometry   3. notice
4. tricky   5. record   6. volunteer

[Review 2]

Conversation 1

Page 145

Woman - Student	Man - Professor
• Failed <u>group project</u> • Spent a lot of <u>time and are discouraged</u> • One member kept <u>interrupting and interfered with progress</u> • <u>He isn't majoring in that program</u> • <u>He's the reason they couldn't get the work done</u>	• Liked their theme but <u>they failed to develop it</u> • If they expanded <u>on ideas then would have passed</u> • <u>It's too late</u> • <u>When in the real world you won't get to choose who you work with</u> • <u>A review is soon, so can get better grades then</u>

1. A   2. C   3. C   4. B

Lecture 1

Page 146-147

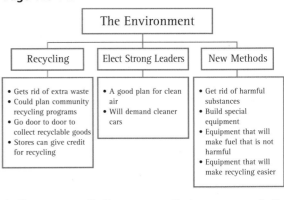

1. C   2. C   3. A   4. C
5. B   6. B

Lecture 2

Page 148-149

Bird Flu

Symptoms	See Doctor	Treatment
• Similar to regular flu • Fever, cough, sore throat, and muscle aches • May be eye infections and pneumonia	• Will perform examination • A special test is needed to find bird flu	• Not much different from regular flu • Same drugs • Bird flu might change • Doctor may send to hospital • Rest and drink lots of water

1. C   2. A   3. D   4. B
5. B   6. C

Lecture 3

Page 150-151

Cause	Effect
• Large ship sank off Alaska • 40 million liters of oil escaped	• Killed many animals • Hurt economy
• Clean up not quick or easy • Machines not good	• New machines invented
• New Grooved oil skimmer	• Faster and easier clean up
• Countries agreed to lend oil skimmers to other countries	• Best way to keep oceans clean and safe

1. B   2. C   3. A   4. D
5. A   6. D

Conversation 2

Page 152

Man - Student	Woman - University Employee
• Would like to change <u>dorm rooms</u> • Roommate never <u>cleans up, they have different schedules</u> • Dirty dishes from <u>cafeteria all over floor</u> • <u>Roommate promises he will be considerate but nothing changes</u> • <u>Can't afford to move out</u> • <u>Needs to improve grades and study in a cleaner, quieter place</u>	• Asks if the roommate has <u>broken any rules</u> • <u>Asks if they have talked and maybe work out a compromise</u> • <u>Will talk to the dorm manager</u>

1. C   2. A   3. B
4. Student, Roommate, Student, Roommate

The computer disk included with this material is for your convenience on an "as is" basis without warranty. The PPLD shall have no liability to any person or entity with respect to any liability, loss or damage caused or alleged to be caused directly or indirectly by the instructions contained in this book or by the computer software and hardware contained or described herein.